Amish Faith

By Sarah Price

The Pennsylvania Dutch used in this manuscript is taken from the Pennsylvania Dutch Revised Dictionary (1991) by C. Richard Beam, Brookshire Publications, Inc. in Lancaster, PA.

Contact the author at on Facebook at
http://www.facebook.com/fansofsarahprice or
visit her Web Blog at http://www.sarahpriceauthor.com.

Price Publishing, LLC.
Morristown, NJ
http://www.pricepublishing.org

Other Books by Sarah Price

The Amish of Lancaster Series
#1: Fields of Corn
#2: Hills of Wheat
#3: Pastures of Faith
#4: Valley of Hope

The Amish of Ephrata Series
#1: The Tomato Patch
#2: The Quilting Bee
#3: The Hope Chest
#4: The Clothes Line (Summer 2013)

The Plain Fame Trilogy
Plain Fame
Plain Change
Plain Again (Summer 2013)

Other Amish Christian Romances
Amish Circle Letters
Amish Circle Letters II
A Gift of Faith: An Amish Christmas Story
An Amish Christmas Carol: Amish Christian Classic Series
A Christmas Gift for Rebecca: An Amish Christian Romance

The Adventures of a Family Dog Series
#1: A Small Dog Named Peek-a-boo
#2: Peek-a-boo Runs Away
#3: Peek-a-boo's New Friends
#4: Peek-a-boo and Daisy Doodle (2013)

Other Books, Novellas and Short Stories
Gypsy in Black
Postcards from Abby (with Ella Stewart)
Meet Me in Heaven (with Ella Stewart)
The Prayer Chain Series (with Ella Stewart)
Mark Miller's One Volume 11: The Power of Faith

Dedication

To Sparrow.
...for being the "bestest" friend
who has brought amazing grace into our home.
This one's for you!
<3

After David had finished talking with Saul, Jonathan became one in spirit with David, and he loved him as himself. ² From that day Saul kept David with him and did not let him return home to his family. ³ And Jonathan made a covenant with David because he loved him as himself. ⁴ Jonathan took off the robe he was wearing and gave it to David, along with his tunic, and even his sword, his bow and his belt.

I Samuel 18: 1-3

Then Jonathan said to David, "Go in peace, since we have both sworn in the name of the LORD, saying, "May the LORD be between you and me, and your descendants and my descendants, forever." So David got up and departed and Jonathan went to his own city.
I Samuel 20:42

Table of Contents

Prologue

Faith stood at the graveyard, the cold wind whipping through her black shawl. She stood with her hand resting protectively upon her stomach as she stared at the tombstone. It was bland. Just a simple, white stone with no special wording: a name, date of birth, date of death. That was it. No designs or markings. No special endearments. The beige colored grass that grew up alongside the stone only bespoke of the time that had already passed. Not enough to forget but just enough to not always remember.

Death, Faith thought, *is as cold as the winter air.*

Indeed, it was cold outside, with the wind whipping through her black cape and skirt. But she barely noticed it. Instead, she was shrouded in the warmth of the memory of her friend: Rebecca Petersheim. The cold winter air that chilled Faith's bones did nothing to cool the heat of her pounding heart.

Not a day passed without her thinking about Rebecca. To forget her friend was simply impossible. In truth, Rebecca's presence surrounded Faith every second of the day. There were days when she imagined Rebecca standing nearby, smiling in approval at Faith's life, a life that Rebecca had unknowingly created for her with one simple request.

Yes, it was impossible to forget Rebecca. Her smile was etched in Faith's memory. Her laughter still rang in her ears. The memories of their friendship seemed to replay like a movie in her mind.

Yet, despite knowing that she would never forget Rebecca, Faith knew that it was becoming increasingly easy to overlook the fact that everything she had was *because* of Rebecca and that promise made, oh so many years ago! A promise born from innocence and cemented in a time of grief. A promise that, against all odds, Faith had kept and, despite these odds, realized that it had been more of a gift than a promise after all.

The sky was overcast and grey. The trees were dark, their bare limbs reaching in unison upward toward the sky. The perfect backdrop to add to the emotion that Faith was feeling. She glanced upward and stared, for just one short moment, at the darkening clouds. It smelled like snow. The year's last snowfall. She wasn't looking forward to it, just like she hadn't been looking forward to visiting Rebecca's grave either. Perhaps her friend's death was still too fresh in her memory.

Turning her attention back to the grey stone, she sighed. It was surrounded by others that looked just like it: A field of identical stones that marked the passing of lives. Some of the stones were old and worn out. A few were fresh, too fresh, attesting of the recent passing of fathers, mothers, and children.

Her eyes locked onto Rebecca's stone. The chiseled words seemed cold and unfriendly. No tender words of endearment that might proclaim that Rebecca had been a beloved wife, a loving mother, a cherished daughter and a dear friend.

Ten months had passed. Ten long months in which entire worlds had shifted. Without Rebecca, life had changed for so many and in so many ways. Oh, Faith knew she should rejoice in the fact that Rebecca walked with the Lord. But the truth was that she missed her friend. She missed her smile and the energy of her youth, her love and adoration of family as a young woman, wife and mother, and her strength and determination in her final years.

How had it come to this, she pondered.

Chapter One

They were six and seven when they first met.

As Faith's father needed a new milking machine for his dairy barn, he had taken her to a farm auction. Their neighbor, Jonas Yoder, had encouraged her father to join him at the Amish auction that was being held on the upcoming Saturday at a nearby farm. Public auctions were always a great place to buy inexpensive, if slightly used, farm equipment.

Faith had stood by her father's side, pulling her brown coat closed at the neck and adjusting the blue headscarf that her mother had forced her to wear. She was not used to being in such a large crowd of Amish men. To Faith, all these men looked similar, with their battered straw hats, white shirts, and black pants held up by black suspenders. Most had long, greying beards and stern expressions on their faces. They didn't look friendly at all.

For a moment, Faith had wished that she hadn't agreed to go with her father. It would have been much more fun staying home, playing in the hayloft or even helping her mother with the chores. Anything but being here with all of these men who spoke in a language she didn't understand and seemed to look right through her as if she didn't exist.

"I know you!" someone exclaimed behind her.

Faith turned around and looked at the girl standing opposite her. She appeared to be about the same age as Faith, despite being a bit taller. She, too, wore a heavy coat and a headscarf but there was something different about her.

"You live on the farm next to ours! The Landes farm!"

the girl said, a big smile lighting her face. "But you don't go to my school, ain't so? How come?"

Faith had only started school that past fall. She went to the public school, a small yellow bus picking her up every day at the end of the driveway. Each morning, her mother would walk with her to the mailbox, waiting with her as they sung a hymn from their church or practiced Faith's spelling. "Cat? Dog? Bat?" Faith would recite the correct spelling of each word, glorifying in the approval of her mother when she got each one correct. "My smart girl," her mother would say and give her a big hug before the bus came.

"I don't know," Faith said to the girl who stood so close to her. She wasn't used to such forwardness from other children, especially strange ones that she didn't really know.

"It wonders me," the girl went on, tapping a dirty finger on the side of her cheek. "Mayhaps you aren't Amish?"

Faith shook her head.

"What are you, then?" the girl asked, the curiosity in her dark eyes more than apparent.

"Mennonite," Faith whispered, wondering if the little girl would still want to talk to her.

"Ja vell," the girl said. "My name's Rebecca. We should be friends, don't you think? We live next to each other and, even if you ain't Amish, we could still play together!"

Faith didn't know how to respond. Rebecca talked funny. Her words sounded like a song with a funny accent. Instead of saying 'other', it came out 'oo-dher'. Instead of saying 'could', she said 'coou-d.' Faith liked the way Rebecca drew out her words. She wished that she could speak like that. "I guess sooo," Faith answered, trying to imitate Rebecca's accent.

Rebecca laughed, her eyes crinkling into small half-moons, and shook her head. "You don't sound Amish at all."

Faith blushed and lowered her eyes, embarrassed.

"What's your name, then?" the girl asked, her eyes sparkling.

"Faith."

For a second, Rebecca frowned. Faith wondered why. Her parents had named her that after years of trying to have a baby. They prayed for a baby, just one. And when her mother had finally learned that she was pregnant, they immediately knew that, if the baby was a girl, they would name her Faith for they had put their faith in God to bring them this one simple request: a healthy, living baby. Faith had never thought twice about her name. Now, however, as Rebecca hesitated and studied Faith, she couldn't help but wonder if something was wrong with her name?

But, just as quick as the frown had appeared, it vanished. Rebecca shrugged and grabbed Faith's hand. "Come on, then. Let's go watch the auction!" Dragging Faith through the sea of Amish men, Rebecca pulled her toward the railing and stood by her side.

For a while, they watched the different pieces of equipment come to the front of the area set aside for the merchandise, the podium and the auctioneer. His voice was barely understandable as he rambled about each item, calling for bids on each piece, and pointing into the crowd whenever people raised their hands. Faith thought the auctioneer was singing and shut her eyes, listening to the magical voice.

She felt someone nudge past her and opened her eyes, seeing a large Amish man push her backward, blocking her view. Faith glanced at Rebecca who frowned, not liking the fact that she could no longer see. But, just as quickly, Rebecca raised her eyebrows and her mouth formed a perfect O, something humorous having caught her attention.

She grabbed at Faith's arm. "Look at that!" she whispered, pointing toward the man in front of her. "He has a piece of toilet paper on his backside!"

Faith looked and started giggling.

Rebecca giggled, too. "Reckon my mamm would want me to tell him but I'm not going to! Serves him right for blocking the view from us!"

From that moment on, Faith knew that Rebecca was going to be her once-in-a-lifetime friend, that special someone whom she would share everything with...secrets, dreams, and mischievous plans. Staring at her new friend, Faith was amazed. How was it possible that this wonderful girl had lived next to her for all of her life and that only now they had just found each other?

Faith never quite understood why she went to a different school than Rebecca. After all, they lived right next to each other. Still, almost every day before evening chores, they would meet in the pasture between their houses and explore the fields, hunting for bird nests in the spring, baby bunnies in the early summer, and pretty butterflies in the waning days of August. They would collect wild flowers and bring them home to their mothers.

Faith was now nine and Rebecca was ten. They spent as much time together as they could, never noticing the differences between them or simply not caring to be bothered by them.

One day, they sat on a picnic table outside of the Yoder's house, looking at the flowers they had collected. It was a Saturday afternoon. A buggy pulled into the driveway and two young men got out, nodding in the direction of the two girls. Faith stared and Rebecca waved as she called out, "Hullo Jacob! Hullo Manuel!"

"Your bruder James around, then?" the older of the two boys said.

"Ja, ja!" Rebecca responded and looked over her shoulder toward the house. "Mayhaps inside, taking a short nap."

The boys walked toward the house, the younger one pausing to peer over Rebecca's shoulder, his eyes sparkling and an inquisitive look on his face. "What you have there, Rebecca?"

She smiled, pointing at the flowers that were spread upon the wooden tabletop. "Pretty, ain't so? Faith and I...well, we're going to press them so we have them forever." Pausing, she glanced at Faith. "Faith, this is Manuel," she said absentmindedly.

Faith flushed and couldn't meet his eyes. They were so blue and bright, as if the prettiest summer sky was reflected there. And his smile lit up his face. She thought that he was the most handsome boy she'd ever seen in her life.

Oblivious to what Faith was thinking, Manuel held out his hand, being a proper young Amish man, and waited until she took it. He shook it and smiled, a brilliant white smile, his blues eyes staring into her brown ones. "Nice to meet you, Faith. Unusual name, that," he said.

"Thanks, Manny," she whispered.

Rebecca frowned. "Manny? Did you call him Manny?"

Annoyed, she shook her head and corrected Faith. "It's *Manuel!*"

Manuel teasingly cuffed Rebecca's head. "Aw, she can call me Manny. I think I right like that," he said. Then, winking at Faith to let her know that her blunder was fine by him, he hurried down the path toward the house. She couldn't help herself from staring after him, surprised at his sparkling blue eyes that had twinkled when she had called him Manny instead of Manuel. And he had winked at her with such a smile on his face, a smile that made her heart flutter.

Once the door shut behind the two boys, Rebecca lost no time to turn and reprimand Faith. "We don't use nicknames, Faith."

"I'm sorry," Faith responded, feeling stupid for the first time in Rebecca's presence. "I didn't know."

"Ja vell, now you do," Rebecca said sharply, turning her attention back to the flowers. "Now, you pick one and I'll pick one. We'll go back and forth, taking turns. That way it's fair and we can each keep our favorite flowers forever." She looked up at Faith and smiled, the nickname incident already forgotten. "Like our friendship, ja?"

Faith smiled back, feeling better already. "Yes," she agreed. "We'll always be friends."

Rebecca reached out and placed her hand atop of Faith's. "I don't have no same-age sister. But I think you are just as good for that, ain't so?"

Without any further words, the two girls began selecting their flowers with Faith picking first because she was younger. When they had their collections sorted, they carried them into the kitchen where Rebecca's mamm would help the girls press the flowers between small pieces of wax paper in the family Bible.

"Come on," Rebecca cried out, waving to Faith as the children ran down the hill toward the pond. "It's going to be fun!"

Oh ja, Faith thought. *Fun for you. You're the one that knows how to swim!* She dreaded the thought of letting the other children know that her parents had never taught her how to swim. She was already eleven years old, a farmer's daughter, who knew little else than how to milk a cow and do well in school. Other than that, Faith was lost.

She was an only child, not for lack of her parents' trying. They had other children but none of them lived past infancy. Two had died in childbirth, the cords wrapped horrendously around their necks, and one had died six months after birth. Only Faith had survived and that had driven her parents to do very little with her. She was never allowed to do anything that might present a hazard. Swimming? Never. Ice-skating? Out of the question! But having fun with the Amish neighbors' children? That seemed harmless enough.

She never had to ask her parents twice. Not when it came to spending time with Rebecca Yoder. Sweet, petite Rebecca with her freckled face and big brown eyes that always seemed to be looking for the next adventure. Leave it to Rebecca to find the nest of abandoned newborn bunnies and undertake the mission of saving them. Count on Rebecca to find a way to make weeding the garden a fun game. Even rainy days were exciting when Rebecca was around. Exciting, but safe.

Yet, Faith was now faced with a great decision as she

stood on the hill overlooking the pond on Rebecca Yoder's uncle's farm. It bordered on Rebecca's place and was a popular swimming destination with the other children. Faith had never ventured there, knowing that she couldn't swim. But Rebecca, her dearest and "bestest" friend ever, had begged her to come along today. And so she had obliged.

Now, Faith was sorry that she had permitted herself to fall prey to peer pressure.

"I don't know," she started to say, trying to mask her reluctance. She didn't want to look scared in front of her friends. "I bet my dad needs my help on the farm with the cows..."

Rebecca rolled her eyes and hurried back to her friend, grabbing her hand and dragging her down the hill. "Don't be silly, goose! It's too early to milk the cows and too hot to not take a quick dip!"

After all of these years, these years growing up together as sisters more than friends, Faith wondered how it was that Rebecca didn't know that she couldn't swim. How had she avoided this in the past? An even better question was how had she not avoided it today?

Even though they were both eleven years old, Rebecca was always quick to point out that she was eight months older than Faith. As far as Amish youth went, Rebecca was different. Quite different. In fact, Faith's parents often laughed that the stork flew over their house by accident and delivered Rebecca to the wrong house.

It was true.

Faith was quiet and reserved, not known for her tomboyish activities. She didn't like getting dirty but was never one to complain to Rebecca about it. Instead, she quietly went along with Rebecca who was a complete take-charge kind of girl. And always, she was smiling and laughing. It was this one particular characteristic that really stuck out about her. "Happy, smiling, laughing Rebecca", she was called.

And everyone loved her.

Especially Faith.

So, strictly because she didn't want to disappoint her friend, Faith let Rebecca lead her down the hill toward the pond and, without a single additional protest, followed her friend into the water.

She hadn't expected the mud to swallow up her legs. Nor did she expect to lose her balance as she tried to trudge behind Rebecca who was already drenched from the waist down and splashing the other children, all boys of different ages. No other girls were in the pond. Just Rebecca and Faith. They were all laughing and having fun, enjoying the cool water that soothed their hot skin under the afternoon sun. All of them except Faith.

She stumbled in the water and, with a pounding heart, fell forward, face first into the murky water. Within seconds, her head was submerged and she slid further down the muddy embankment, completely losing her way. Terrified, she tried to call out but all that happened was water rushing into her mouth and down her throat. Her eyes were wide open and she could barely see anything for the other children had churned up the otherwise clear water.

This is it, she thought. I'm going to drown.

She began to feel lightheaded and the darkness began to grow. She felt herself slipping into a deep abyss and realized, with stunning clarity, that she actually felt at peace, comfortable and warm. Her body felt light and her fear began to subside. No longer did she fight the feeling that she was being embraced and held back from escaping. Instead, she succumbed to it with grace and dignity.

"Come on, Faith!"

The voices seemed to be far away. Too far away. And everything was still dark.

"Manuel! Do something!"

That sounded like Rebecca except her voice was strange. Panicking. Fearful. Upset. Faith had never heard her sound like that; not happy-go-lucky Rebecca! For a moment, Faith wondered what had made Rebecca so frantic.

"You have to save her, Manuel! Save her!"

"Come on, come on," a male voice begged, desperation in his voice.

As if in a moment of electric force, the light came back but it was too bright. The sounds were louder. In fact, all of her senses were heightened, especially the pressure on her lips and nose. Someone was pinching her nose and someone was pressing their mouth against hers, breathing life back into her still body. One Mississippi, two Mississippi, three Mississippi. She felt a pressure on her chest before it returned to her lips.

Her eyes fluttered open and she immediately focused on the blue eyes, hovering above hers. Dark, deep-set eyes with an intensity that burned through her. She felt his lips against hers, forcing her mouth open again. As she began to make sense of what was happening, she began to cough and sputter, water being released from her lungs. She felt someone pull her upwards and pound her on her back. Feeling weak and lifeless, she leaned against someone's shoulder, her cheek pressed against the rough, wet cloth of a man's shirt.

"Faith!"

Again, it was Rebecca.

Faith shut her eyes and tried to take a deep breath. Fresh air had never tasted so pure and clean. "What happened?" she choked out, her words barely audible.

"You almost drowned."

Faith tried to pull back and look at the man who said that. Vaguely, she recognized him. Manuel Petersheim. One of the older Amish boys that she sometimes saw at the different gatherings. She knew him to be seventeen and that was about it. When she realized that she was in his arms, she tried to push away but couldn't. His arms were wrapped around her, holding her up.

"It's alright," he soothed. "Take a deep breath."

She listened to him and tried to relax.

"Oh Manuel!" Rebecca gushed, her voice cracking. Faith realized that her friend was crying. "You saved her!"

"What happened?" Faith repeated.

Manuel pulled back, still keeping a close hold on her. He stared at her, taking in her blue eyes and wet hair. Shaking his head, he tried to smile but his face was pale, the color drained from it. "Seems like someone thought she could float, ja?" He tilted his head, just a touch, and raised an eyebrow. "Mayhaps next time you might take a swimming lesson or two before you venture into water."

Before Faith could respond, Rebecca was on her knees and had her arms around her friend, crying as she hugged her. "You goose! Why didn't you tell me you couldn't swim?"

The images came back to her. The water. The mud. Sinking. That was when she began to shake. Indeed, as she realized that she had almost drowned, her own tears began to fall down her face. Her hands shook, her body shook. She just wanted to go home. To be in her mother's kitchen, wrapped in her embrace. "I want to go home," she managed to utter between her sobs.

"I'll take you home," Manuel said. "My buggy's over there. Come, Rebecca. You ride along and show me where she lives, ja?"

The three of them walked across the field, Rebecca and Manuel on either side of Faith, helping to support her. The other children watched from the side of the pond, still speechless from having just watched the almost drowning of Faith Landes, the Englische friend of Rebecca Yoder. Quietly, all of them quickly gathered their things and walked back over the field, away from that pond and to the safety of their own parents' farms.

As soon as Rebecca turned sixteen, she started what was called her *rumschpringe*, the time when Amish youths are allowed to explore the world of the Englische. She explained this to Faith with great excitement as she prepared to attend her very first singing on a Sunday evening. Her older brother was going to take her and Rebecca could hardly contain her enthusiasm. After all, she told Faith, she was now considered an adult. The idea of being able to socialize with her Amish friends and be worldlier made Rebecca's eyes sparkle.

"But you already know the world of the Englische," Faith said glumly as she sat on the edge of Rebecca's bed. "You know it through me."

Rebecca was pinning on her apron over her dress, expertly sliding the straight pins through the black fabric without looking. "I know that, goose! But this is *different*!"

"I can't see how," Faith pointed, not liking the fact that Rebecca was going somewhere where she couldn't go as well. "It's a singing. It's not even Englische!"

At that, Rebecca laughed, the sound like sweet music. Usually whenever Rebecca laughed, Faith would join in. It was contagious. Just not this time. "I'm sixteen now," she tried to explain. "I can court young men if I want to!"

Faith made a face. Court men? There was nothing further from her mind than getting involved with boys. Her parents wouldn't dream of letting her court anyone. They had forbidden such a thing, saying that courting invited trouble, although Faith suspected it was just one more way to keep her protected and safe. Still, she didn't mind. "Courting leads to marriage, Rebecca. And you know where *that* leads you..."

Waving her hand over her shoulder, Rebecca turned to look at the small hand-held mirror that she picked up from the top of her small, narrow dresser. "I know, I know," she mumbled, pinching her cheeks so that they were rosy pink.

"Babies!" Faith said, making a face. "Yuck."

Rebecca sighed and set the mirror back onto the dresser. "Now Faith," she said, turning around with one hand on her hip. "You know how I feel about that," she said sharply.

It was true. Faith did know exactly how her friend felt about babies. Rebecca came from a large family. She had nine siblings, five older and four younger. She had over 150 cousins, many of whom she had never even met. Family gatherings at the Yoder household usually meant over 200 people in attendance. Much different than Faith's own extended family of only thirty people.

Truth was that Rebecca adored children. Truth was that Rebecca longed for the day when she would have her own farm and raise her own family. Truth was that Faith couldn't even imagine not finishing high school and, hopefully, attending the local community college so that she could find a nice job and stand on her own two feet, even if that included still living at home with her parents. It was one, if not the only way that the two young women differed.

Faith flopped back onto the bed and tossed her arm over her eyes. "Oh, go ahead and find your young Amish man, get married, and have your twenty children."

She felt something soft hit her in the face and sat up, leaning on her elbows. Rebecca was frowning at her but it was a teasing frown. It was a rare moment when Rebecca was truly angry or upset. Faith looked around and saw that her friend had tossed a balled up handkerchief at her. "Twenty children, for sure and certain," Rebecca scoffed playfully.

When it was time for Rebecca to leave, her brother James motioned for Faith to join them in his buggy. He offered to drop her off at her parents' farm. Faith shook her head, needing the time to walk and clear her head. She stood in the driveway, watching as the buggy pulled away, feeling as if a part of their friendship was disappearing with it.

"I have big news, Rebecca!"

Faith could hardly contain herself. She had received the letter earlier that week but hadn't had time to speak to her friend. As busy seventeen year olds, they only found time for visiting on Saturday afternoons. Faith was busy with high school and Rebecca often went to market on Thursdays and Fridays, leaving the house at dawn and returning after seven in the evening. On Saturday mornings, they both had chores to do around the house, especially with spring just around the corner.

"I have big news, too!" Rebecca said, her tone more solemn than usual.

Gone was the vivacious Rebecca that Faith had grown to love over the years. But Faith barely noticed as she gushed her announcement.

"I'm going to college!"

She had received the letter from Frank and Marshall College in Lancaster, not just accepting her into the next freshman class on early admission but also offering her a much-needed scholarship. Faith had never thought that she'd be able to go to a four-year institution. She had always planned on attending the local community college. It had been her guidance counselor that had encouraged her to try harder and reach higher. After all, Mrs. Pierce had argued, Faith was a straight-A student. Why settle for a community college when scholarships might be available to larger, more well-known academic institutions?

"Can you believe it? Frank and Marshall accepted me! I'm going to study English Literature!" Faith was all but hugging herself with delight. "And I'm able to start next year. I'm graduating high school a year early!"

"That's right gut," Rebecca said but her eyes seemed distant and unfocused. College was a foreign entity to Rebecca. After all, she had stopped attending school in the eighth grade. She knew the basics: reading, writing, and arithmetic with a little bit of geography and history tossed in there. But that was all she needed to know to survive in the world of the Amish.

"Aren't you excited for me?"

Rebecca tried to smile but Faith knew that the true

importance was lost on her friend.

It had been this way for a while. As Faith matured and became part of her own world, Rebecca seemed to dissolve into hers. The chasm between their two worlds was increasing. Faith recognized it. Rebecca was aware of it. But they both continued trying to deny it existed.

Sighing, Faith gave up. "OK, so what's your big news then?"

At this, Rebecca lit up. Her face glowed and her eyes sparkled. For a moment, Faith saw her old friend, her "bestest" buddy enticing her to climb a tree or build a dam in the stream in the pasture. "I'm going to take my instructional."

Faith frowned. Instructional? That wasn't what she had expected Rebecca to say. Without being told, Faith knew what 'take my instructional' meant. It meant that Rebecca would take twelve weeks of lessons from the bishop prior to being able to become a baptized member of the church. Faith also knew that once Rebecca took that kneeling vow, promising to honor the Amish faith and traditions, both old and new, there was no turning back. The Amish culture and the Amish religion were different, true. But once someone became a baptized member, it was one and the same.

"Oh."

Now it was Rebecca's turn to frown. "Is that all you can say? 'Oh'? This is a big step for me."

Faith didn't know how to respond. A big step? She failed to see how that was true. After all, Rebecca's parents had been grooming her for this next step, the same way other children took communion at other churches. "Well, that's great, Rebecca," she managed to say, although she wasn't quite certain that she meant it. "We always knew you would take the kneeling vow."

Appeased, Rebecca nodded eagerly. "I had to pray long and hard on it, Faith. I wasn't certain if this year was the right year but," she paused, her eyes glancing into the distance. Something else was on her mind, something that seemed to create an inner glow. "Ja, it's the right time."

There was a peace about Rebecca's face as she said these words. Faith could only watch in amazement and wonder, amazed that her friend was so determined and certain of herself and wondering if she, too, might one day feel the same way.

"What do you mean, you're getting married?"

In complete disbelief, Faith stared at her friend. Rebecca lowered her eyes. Faith wasn't certain whether Rebecca was being demure about the subject or was merely uncomfortable discussing this with her. If Faith had learned anything about the Amish over the past few years, it was how private they were about such things as courtship and marriage.

Yet, there was something else at play. Faith had noticed an increasing distance between them. The more Rebecca clung to the Amish faith and lifestyle, the further apart they became. However, this gap had increased significantly in the past six months, which, Faith suspected, was probably about the time when her friend had begun to seriously court Manuel Petersheim.

"I'd like you to come to the wedding," Rebecca finally asked. "It's in two weeks on Thursday at my mamm's house."

Faith's mouth fell open. "Two weeks? That's not much of an engagement!"

Rebecca lifted her eyes and stared at Faith, no words slipping through her lips in response.

"You just took your baptism! You just turned eighteen!"

"Ja?" The way Rebecca said it could easily have been translated into '*So What?*'

"Ja?" Faith repeated in disbelief. "Ja? That's all you can say?" But what she was really thinking was: *How did this happen? How had we drifted so far apart?* "Wow, Rebecca," she finally went on. "I guess I should just say congratulations and how lucky Manny is."

"Manuel," Rebecca corrected, an edge to her voice. "You need to stop calling him that strange and silly nickname!"

Faith rolled her eyes. "Manuel then."

"He bought a farm," Rebecca gushed, ignoring Faith's reaction. "It's a wunderbaar gut farm with almost 100 acres!" She grabbed Faith's hands. "Can you imagine?"

"No," Faith said, relieved that she could finally be honest with her friend. "No, I cannot."

"It's a bit on a hill," she continued. "But the farmhouse! Oh Faith! I can see it now! Hanging out the laundry from the edge of the porch! The line runs right to the corner of the barn!"

Faith didn't know how to respond. "That...that sounds lovely."

Rebecca wasn't listening and for that, Faith was grateful. She didn't want her friend to hear the hesitation in her voice and her lack of enthusiasm for the big news. Instead, Rebecca gushed on. "Some of the acreage is wooded but at least the potential is there."

"Sounds like it," Faith added, hoping that she sounded sincere.

Rebecca took a deep, satisfied breath. "Can you believe it? After all these years? To think that Manuel Petersheim, the very young man who saved your life years ago, is now going to become my husband?" She clutched her hands together and sighed. "He's so amazingly kind and sweet. And such a good-hearted man. I couldn't be any happier!"

For a moment, Faith felt ashamed of herself. The look of adoration on Rebecca's face made her realize how selfish she had been. Her friend, her lifelong, 'bestest' friend was overjoyed with happiness and all Faith could think about was herself...her own framework and expectations for life. One of the saving graces for their friendship had always been a respectful acceptance of their differences. When had she lost that acceptance for the Amish way of life and Rebecca's upbringing?

Turning to her friend, Faith smiled, a genuine smile as she said, "Oh Rebecca, I think this is just wonderful news!"

It was only ten months later when Faith nervously stood at the door to Rebecca and Manuel's farmhouse. She hesitated before opening it and entering. It had only been a few months back when Faith had been there for the first time. Rebecca and Manuel had just moved in, six months after their wedding. Prior to that, they had lived apart: Rebecca at her parents' farm and Manuel at his parents'. Despite having bought the farm on Musser School Road, the previous owners hadn't moved out yet so, during their first months of marriage, Rebecca and Manuel had lived apart.

Faith hadn't pretended to understand that arrangement but she knew from experience that most newly married Amish couples did not live together. Instead, they visited each other on the weekends, often traveling around the countryside to stay with relatives or share the evening meal with friends. Eventually, usually around springtime, the couple would settle into their first home to begin a life together as a married couple. In the Petersheim's case, Manuel had been fortunate enough to be in a financial position to buy an actual farm. A forever home. Given that he was older, he had saved up enough money since he had turned sixteen in order to purchase the farm at a public auction.

She didn't want to go into the house. She knew exactly what she would see. Her friend, her oldest and "bestest" friend, would have become a true Amish woman. Her dress would be plain, her head covering freshly starched and perched on top of her head, held in place by a single straight pin through the fabric, and she would have a baby held snuggly buggly in her arms.

A baby!

Rebecca had just turned twenty. Already she was a mother.

And Faith knew that her friend would be happy.

"Faith!"

She looked up in the direction of the voice that called out her name from the barn. It was Manuel. He was smiling, the hint of his new beard shadowing his jawbone. His tattered straw was casting a shadow over his face but she could certainly see his smile: Broad, white, and full of joy.

She still felt shy around him. After all of these years, she remembered her near-death experience and waking in his arms, his mouth pressed against hers as his worried eyes examined her face for some sign of life. It hadn't been until a few weeks after that incident that she had learned that Manuel had been driving his buggy down the road and heard Rebecca's scream. The other children had noticed Faith in the water, dragged her to the edge of the pond, luckily the closest point to the road. Seeing the children gathered around the limp body of the Englischer girl, Manuel had quickly assessed what happened, stopped his buggy, and raced across the small swath of grass toward the pond to administer CPR. Where he had learned it, Faith never actually found out. But the fact that his mouth had been pressed against hers, breathing life into her body, saving her soul from floating away forever, had always intimidated her.

"Hello Manny," she said.

He grinned at the nickname that Faith had always used when addressing him, despite Rebecca's insistence that he be called Manuel. "Rebecca will be right pleased to see you! You always have a way of making her shine."

Faith flushed at the compliment.

He shoved his hands into his pants pockets and rocked on his heels, grinning at her. "You here to see the baby, then?"

She nodded.

"She's a real sweet little thing," he affirmed as he bounded up the porch steps and opened the door for her. "And Rebecca is just a most wunderbaar gut mamm!"

No doubt, thought Faith. Rebecca always had a way of doing everything perfectly.

Inside the house, it took a moment for Faith to collect her bearings. The kitchen was dark, the plain green shades having been pulled down to block the hot summer sun. As her eyes adjusted, Faith looked toward the sofa at the back of the kitchen, near the wall that was adjacent to the stairwell. There sat Rebecca, a smile on her face and, as Faith had suspected, a small bundle wrapped in a thin blanket cuddled in her arms.

Faith approached her, not certain of how to react to her friend's in this new role as a mother. At nineteen, Faith barely felt as if she were an adult. To think that her friend was already a wife and now a mother simply left her speechless. It was beyond her imagination to think of these responsibilities at such a young age, even if Rebecca was several months her elder.

"I've come to meet the newest Petersheim," she finally said as she walked toward the sofa. "Let me meet baby Anna!"

Rebecca gestured for Faith to sit next to her on the sofa, shifting slightly so that there was enough room for her friend. "I'm ever so glad you came, Faith! Come meet my *dochder*," she prompted, her voice soft and musical as she moved the baby in her arms so that Faith could see her in the dim light.

And there she was. The perfect little replica of Rebecca, wrapped in a soft yellow cloth. Her eyes were shut but Faith could see that the baby looked exactly like her mother, with a soft button nose, high little forehead, and pursed, determined lips. The baby was simply gorgeous and, at once, Faith understood. She understood everything about her friend and the divide that had grown between them.

While Faith was pursuing her education in the hopes of some day becoming a teacher, Rebecca was pursuing her own passion: being a true and devout Amish woman. That meant being a wife, a mother, and a devout member of the church community.

With one look at the sweet, angelic face of baby Anna in Rebecca's arms, Faith understood for the very first time that the worldly path was not necessarily the better path. What was important in the world was the expression on Rebecca's face as she stared down in complete amazement and adoration at the sleeping infant in her arms.

Faith wished that she could have that same kind of peace and purpose. Her heart suddenly sang with delight for her friend, even though it tugged at her own consciousness. Faith realized that she would probably never have what Rebecca already had and the thought made her immensely sad. How unfortunate, she thought, that the Englische world doesn't understand what is truly important!

"Oh, Rebecca," Faith gasped, reaching out to hold the baby. "She's simply beautiful." And she meant it.

By the time she was twenty-five, Faith had not only graduated from college but landed a teaching position at a nearby Mennonite school. She was happy to live with her parents, thankful that she didn't have to pay rent or share her life with roommates. She much preferred waking up to the sound of cows mulling about, waiting for the morning milking. Her dad was always thankful on those days when Faith woke early in order to assist him. There was nothing she loved more than welcoming the day, the fresh air, clean and brisk, and the light of dawn breaking from dark blue to light grey to pale yellow as the sun crested over the hill of the back paddock.

It had been eight years since Rebecca had married Manuel Petersheim. Since that time, she had welcome five babies into the world: three daughters and two sons. Faith and Rebecca didn't get to see each other very much. During the week, Faith was busy at work, helping the children after school and her father in the evenings. On the weekends, Faith was often occupied grading papers while Rebecca had her hands full with so many kinner under the age of ten to tend to.

The last time Faith had gone visiting, she was surprised to see that the house was not in its usual pristine shape. There were toys scattered on the floor, dirty dishes on the counter, and a pile of laundry that needed to be washed. While Anna, at seven years old, tried to help her mamm, it was too much for one small child to undertake.

"Rebecca," Faith had whispered when the children were out of range to overhear. "Is everything alright?"

She nodded her head but there were tears in her eyes. Faith knew immediately that her friend was not telling her the truth.

"What's wrong, Rebecca?"

Rebecca glanced over at the children, playing in the sunroom with some wooden toys. A tear fell from her eye and she looked back at her friend. "I had another miscarriage last week," she admitted. "I haven't told Manuel."

Faith gasped. Over the years, she had come to respect the relationship between Manuel and Rebecca, loving the easy-going nature of their relationship. If nothing else, they had become a true couple, reading each other's minds, sharing private jokes, and always being there for each other. Faith couldn't imagine why Rebecca would keep something so important from her husband. "Why ever not?" she demanded.

With a gentle shrug, Rebecca tried to dismiss the subject. "He has enough to worry about. He's so busy on the farm and the boys aren't old enough to really help yet. Just a few more years and life will be so much easier for him. I didn't want to burden him," she explained.

Burden him? Faith couldn't believe that she was hearing

these words from her friend's mouth. Manuel would be horrified to know that Rebecca kept such an important secret from him. He would have wanted to be there for her, to help her deal with both the physical stress and the emotional loss. Certainly he would have helped her with the children so that she could have recovered, if such a thing was possible for Rebecca. The loss of a child, even an unborn one, was certainly devastating to someone who doted on all of her children.

"He'd want to know, Rebecca," Faith coaxed gently. "He *needs* to know."

Rebecca shrugged. "And let him know that I can't have anymore children?" The tone of her voice was shockingly depressing. Faith had never heard her sound so down on herself. Not Rebecca. Strong Rebecca. "Promise me something," Rebecca said suddenly, reaching her hand out to grab Faith's.

"Anything," Faith whispered, startled by the gesture.

"If anything ever happens to me," Rebecca started and then paused. She glanced over at the children. "Promise me that you'll be here for them."

"Rebecca!"

"And for Manuel."

"Stop it!" Faith said, snatching her hand away. "Don't talk like that."

Sighing, Rebecca raised her hand to rub her eyes. She was tired and needed to recover, that much Faith could see. But the recovery was more than physical. It was emotional as well. "You know me better than anyone, Faith," Rebecca went on. "I need to know that you would be a part of their lives."

"I'm going to get Manuel," Faith said. "You're talking nonsense!"

"Nee!" She shook her head adamantly, determined to

get an answer to her request. "Just promise me and then we can have a nice visit, ja?"

Faith took a deep breath. She could see the sorrow in her friend's eyes and the longing to hear those words, words that would commit Faith because her word was her bond. But Faith also knew that those words would help her friend heal. Reaching out to hold Rebecca's hand, she stared at her friend and smiled, a sorrowful smile, as she nodded. "I would never abandon your family, Rebecca. You know that."

"So you promise?"

Slowly, the words formed on Faith's lips. "Of course I promise. How could I not?" In a rare moment of emotional relief, Rebecca let Faith embrace her, a friendly embrace that signed their verbal contract, a contract Faith never thought she would have to fulfill, some day.

Faith was twenty-nine when she got the news. She had been in her classroom, cleaning up from the day's lessons when her cell phone rang. It was unusual for anyone to call her at this time for they all knew that she would still be in the classroom. Frowning, she crossed the room and opened the desk drawer where she kept her mobile phone. She dug around until she found it, the light on it glowing blue with the number for her home displaying.

"Hello Mom," she said as she answered, worried. Her mother never called her on the phone and in the middle of the day.

Faith had been teaching for almost seven years, loving each and every moment of it. She taught the fourth graders, and had come to think of all of them as her own children. She loved their wide-eyed innocence, their different and very individual journeys into the world of reading and writing. Some were very advanced while others lagged behind. The challenges motivated Faith and she made certain to tailor each lesson to both layers of learners, as well as those in-between.

Her dedication to her students had hindered her own personal relationships. She hadn't dated very much over the years. Oh, a dinner here and a movie there. But she wasn't interested in the men that seemed to be attracted to her. For Faith, there was something about them that turned her away. They were shallow and materialistic, focusing too much on the future and not on the here and now. They treated her choice of a career as quaint, as though she was biding time until she would get married and have babies of her own. Indeed, it never failed to turn her off from any potentially serious relationship.

She knew that her parents appreciated the fact that she still lived at home. She was able to assist them with the chores around the farm both before and after her own work. As her father aged, he had taken to hiring several local Amish boys to work the fields with him and assist in milking the cows in the morning. But every evening, Faith made certain that she was there, working alongside her father. She had come to believe that it kept her grounded in what was really important.

Now, as she held the phone to her ear, she was worried indeed. Knowing that Faith would soon be on her way home, what could possibly have happened that her mother would call her at this hour? Immediately, she feared the worst: her father, an accident, a heart attack? In that split second of terror, she imagined the future without her father. What would happen to the farm? What would happen to her mother? How would they survive?

"You need to come home now," her mother said, her voice flat and emotionless. "Something's happened."

Faith's heart began to pound inside of her chest. She knew. Just as sure as the sun rose every morning, she knew that her father had a heart attack. She knew that he had pushed himself to the limit. She just prayed that someone had found him quick enough to get him to the hospital. Faith squeezed her eyes shut and braced herself for the news. "Where is he? Is he going to make it?"

Silence.

"Mother?"

"Who?" her mother asked, her tone sharp and edgy. "Is *who* going to make it?"

"Father!" Faith demanded, suddenly angry at her mother for not just spitting out the news and simply telling her whatever was wrong.

Another hesitation. "It's not your father, Faith," her mother finally said. "It's Rebecca."

Faith didn't stop at her parents' farm. Instead, she drove as fast as she could down the back roads to the Petersheim farm. She cursed under her breath when she had to slow down before passing a few horse and buggies. *Move, move, move*, she willed them, silently begging them to move to the side of the road so that she could safely pass and hurry to her friend's side.

There were several buggies in the Petersheim's driveway. That was never a good sign, Faith told herself angrily. Not on a Wednesday. She quickly put her car in park and turned off the ignition before she stumbled out of the car door and raced toward the house.

How had this happened, she asked herself. Why hadn't she stopped trying when the doctor told her? Three miscarriages and one stillborn were enough, the doctor had said. Each loss made Rebecca withdraw more and more until there was just a shell of a woman in there, the hint of the friend that had stubbornly refused to inform that man at the horse auction that he had toilet paper stuck on the back of his pants. In fact, Faith hadn't seen her for almost six months. Their lives had just drifted apart, Rebecca with raising her family and helping Manuel on the farm and Faith raising her own children: her students.

The room was filled with people, many of whom she had never met before. But they were all Amish. Mostly men although there were a few women, standing near the counter, their ashen faces staring at nothing as if in shock. Only one person looked up at Faith when she flew into the room: Manuel. His eyes were wide and frightened. The color was drained from his face. But when he saw Faith, he caught his breath, as if relieved.

"Faith!"

As if prompted, the other men turned in unison to look at her. They were older men, all wearing black suits and black hats. Their faces were void of emotion, stern expressions greeting her. As soon as they focused on her, they immediately turned away. She was, after all, an Englischer; an outsider. But Manuel ignored their coldness and crossed the room to greet Faith. He placed his hand on her arm and guided her toward a door in the back of the room.

"You must go speak to Rebecca," he said softly. "You must speak some sense into her."

"I...I don't understand," Faith whispered, glancing over his shoulder at the frowns on the faces of the other people in the room.

"She won't go to the hospital!"

That was something Faith couldn't understand. "Why ever not?"

Manuel shook his head, tears in his eyes. "Says it's God's will and she won't lose another baby." He opened the door and pleaded with her. "You need to convince her to go, Faith. You are the only one who can do it!" Without another word, he gently pushed Faith into the room and shut the door behind her.

The room was dark but lit up by the glow of several kerosene lanterns. It was the master bedroom that was located on the first floor. Faith's gaze rested on the sweaty, pale figure lying in the middle of the full bed: Rebecca. On either side of her were two Amish women, one that Faith had seen before and thought she might be Manuel's younger sister. The other was Rebecca's mother, her face pale and tears in her eyes. Faith nodded to both of them as she hurried to her friend's side.

"What are you doing, Rebecca? You have everyone quite worried!" Faith tried to sound nonchalant and in control although inside she felt nothing of the sort.

Rebecca forced a weak smile. Her lips were chapped and dry. She reached out a shaky hand for Faith to hold. "You came!"

"Of course I came, goose," Faith said, smiling back at her friend. "Now, why won't you go to the hospital?"

Rebecca shut her eyes. "I want to deliver this baby at home."

Rebecca's mother shook her head. "Stubborn girl! She'll

die delivering this baby!" The other woman met Faith's gaze and nodded her head, affirming what was said.

Faith knelt down and leaned close to Rebecca. "You have to go to the hospital, Rebecca. You can't die. You have five other children and a husband who need you." She paused before adding, "*I* need you."

"Nee," Rebecca said. For a moment, she cringed, her eyes squeezing shut and she lifted herself off the bed. A contraction. When the pain subsided, she gasped for air and managed to whisper, "This baby *will* live."

"Even if it means you won't?" Faith stared at her friend, both admiring and despising her fierce determination.

Rebecca shut her eyes and sank back down into the pillow. She took a few breaths before she finally opened her eyes and looked at Faith, trying to focus on her friend's face. "You..." She paused, not finishing her thought.

"Me what?"

Rebecca clutched Faith's hand, squeezing it as another wave of pain caused her to tighten her body and fight the urge to scream. Out of the corner of her eyes, Faith could see Rebecca's mamm cringe and turn away, fighting her own emotion at the thought of losing her dear dochder. "You..." Rebecca gasped. "You...don't forget your promise, Faith." She struggled as a contraction started. "You take care of my children and...you...help...Manny..." she managed to say.

And then she let out a loud cry, her body rising once again on the bed as she pushed, crushing Faith's hand in the process. The other Amish woman shook her head and moved to the foot of the bed, pushing sheets back and speaking in Pennsylvania Dutch, words that Faith couldn't understand but that caused Rebecca's mamm to cry and turn away.

Within minutes, the baby cried out, a small, bloody baby with a crooked and slightly underdeveloped leg. Despite the deformity, the baby seemed healthy, crying as the midwife quickly wrapped it into a warm blanket and handed it to Faith. The baby forgotten, the midwife turned her attention back to Rebecca, doing what she could to stop the flow of blood that was now coming out of the limp body on the bed. Faith watched, dumbfounded, holding the crying infant as she watched the life seep away from the body of her oldest and "bestest" friend. Rebecca never regained consciousness, never held her baby, and never knew that she had just given birth to her sixth child...a little girl who would never walk, never run, never swim in a pond, and never know the love of her mother or understand the sacrifice Rebecca had just made, trading her own life for this of the little newborn.

Chapter Two

Faith was still holding the baby when the bishop arrived, removing his hat upon entering the kitchen. Manuel was standing in the kitchen, his face drawn and pale, never once even looking at the newborn baby that had just cost him a wife. Instead, he stared at the floor, a look of complete disbelief in his eyes. No one spoke. The room had been silent for almost twenty minutes, the only noise coming from the bundle in Faith's arms...soft, mewing sounds from the baby girl.

It had been the midwife who had finally lifted up her eyes and, meeting Faith's pleading stare, shaking her head in disbelief before she backed away from the bed. Rebecca's mamm had let out a loud wail, almost falling to her knees against the bedframe but the midwife had caught her and sat her on the chair next to the nightstand.

"Why? Why?" Rebecca's mother had yelled, her voice choked with sorrow and pain.

Faith tore her eyes from Rebecca's mamm and stared back at the lifeless body of her friend. The color was gone from Rebecca's cheeks. So was the pain that had accompanied her out of this world. Instead, the look on her departed friend's face was one of peace and relief. Faith took a deep breath, forcing herself not to cry. How could she when Rebecca had done exactly what she wanted? She had given her life for her child, for this precious bundle that she now held in her arms. The alternative had been to take the child but spare the mother and Rebecca would never have been able to live with herself after making such a choice.

The door had opened and, without a word, Manuel walked in. No one had needed to tell him what had happened. He had known from the cry of grief that escaped his mother-in-law's lips. Rebecca had died. She walked with the Lord. But that was not enough comfort for a man left a widower at thirty-eight with six children, one a newborn with a physical deformity. One look at his face told Faith all that she needed to know. Manuel Petersheim would much rather have his wife alongside him, to help with the farm work, to raise their children, and to grow old together than to have her walk with the Lord.

Where is that strong Amish faith now, Faith had asked herself, too aware of the bitterness in her thought.

"It's a girl," she had managed to whisper, not knowing what else to say.

Manuel had barely acknowledged what Faith had said. Instead, he had stared at the body of his wife. His eyes took in the blood stained sheets, which, despite her best efforts, the mid-wife hadn't been able to completely cover. He took two steps toward the bed, pausing to rest his hand on the shoulder of Rebecca's mamm. In response, she had lifted her own hand to cover his, the only comfort either one would most likely receive over the next few days.

"Best be fetching the bishop," Manuel had mumbled, looking at the mid-wife as he assigned her the task of telling the others that were crowded in the kitchen. Then, he had moved to the side of the bed and sat down, the movement gentle and careful, as if not to awaken Rebecca. For the next fifteen minutes, he had sat with his wife, holding her hand and staring into her face.

Faith had stood there, uncertain of what to do as she

had watched Rebecca's mamm leave the room and slowly walk into the kitchen. She headed over to where the clock was on the mantel by the fireplace. Without a word, she had reached up and stopped the clock. It was frozen at 4:49pm. When the clock had stopped ticking, the other women in the kitchen had begun to quietly cry. The men had removed their hats and stood there, silent as they all bowed their heads in prayer.

Now, as the bishop had finally arrived, everyone was standing in the kitchen, waiting for direction from their leader. Faith stood in the shadows, feeling out of place in the gathering of men dressed in black and women in simple, plain dresses. Her own dress, a soft blue sleeveless dress with a small floral pattern, stuck out among the Amish. It screamed outsider...Englischer...and made Faith feel even more uncomfortable.

She glanced around the room, noticing that Manuel was still standing at the back of the kitchen, alone and staring at the floor with a despondent look upon his ashen face. Indeed, his eyes were blank, large and distant. For a moment, Faith watched him, concerned about his reaction and how he would handle this unexpected change in his life. How would he manage without Rebecca? The thought seemed so surreal and foreign to Faith that she found herself feeling as if everything was just a bad dream.

The whimpering noise from the bundle in her arms told Faith that, indeed, this was not a bad dream, not just a nightmare. No, Rebecca had died and here she was, standing in the kitchen of the Petersheim residence, holding a newborn baby. She wondered why no one had tended to the baby, yet. She had no idea about what to do with a newborn infant. Her experience with babies was limited. In fact, she had never even babysat before and the only time she had held a baby was when she had visited Rebecca, when each one of her friend's children had been born. Now, she was holding a newborn baby, one that hadn't even been properly cleaned yet, as everyone was still in shock that their vivacious, loving, energetic Rebecca had just passed away. Died. Gone.

"Let us pray," the bishop finally said. As if on command, everyone dropped to their knees and leaned against a chair or sofa, their hands cupped together and pressed against their foreheads in fervent, silent prayer. Faith stood there, watching and wishing that someone would tell her what to do. Of all the experiences Rebecca had shared with her, death had not been one of them.

Faith stared around the room, taking in the image of fifteen people, kneeling on the floor of Rebecca's kitchen, their heads bent respectfully in prayer while she stood there, feeling her own sense of shock for having witnessed the birth of a new life at the same time as the life of another human being had been swept away.

"Please," Faith heard herself utter when the people finally stood up. Her voice sounded strained and distant. She barely recognized it herself. "Please, could someone help me with this baby?"

One of the other women caught her breath and hurried over to Faith's side. Quietly, the woman guided Faith and the bundle in her arms to another room, away from the mourners and away from Rebecca's body. With expert hands, the woman took the baby from Faith and gently unswaddled it. For a moment, she seemed to pause as she took in the sight of the deformed leg but, almost as quickly, she regained her composure and nodded her head.

"We'll be needing some warm water, then," she instructed Faith. "And a clean cloth, ja? You know where Rebecca keeps them?"

Present tense. As if Rebecca had just gone out to the store.

Faith shook her head. The woman, who Faith now recognized as Rebecca's sister-in-law, Lydia, clicked her tongue and, tucking the blanket back around the infant, motioned for Faith to watch. Then, without another word, Lydia disappeared into the large washroom that was on the other side of the kitchen to fetch the items that she needed.

The baby mewed softly in Faith's arms, almost like a small kitten. Her pouty mouth opened slightly and a tiny pink tongue poked out. Tears came to Faith's eyes and she fought the urge to cry, to really let the tears fall down her cheeks and succumb to the grief she felt. She felt her heart swell with love for the baby while resenting it at the same time. The birth of this child, this beautiful child of Christ, had cost Rebecca her life.

Faith couldn't help but wonder, *Can such a horrific sacrifice ever make any sense?*

The next few days seemed surreal to Faith. She had taken a leave of absence from work, wanting to help as much as she could with the preparations for Rebecca's funeral. Of course, there wasn't that much to do. The Amish community had swung into action, members of the church district immediately taking over the tasks of tending to the children, cleaning the house, preparing the food, and even digging the grave in the cemetery. In reality, there wasn't much at all for

Faith to do.

Manuel's sister had taken over the care of the infant, whom, as of the day of the funeral service, was still unnamed. The other children seemed to be in shock, but coping better than Manuel, all of them save Anna. At almost twelve years of age, the loss of a mother was extra painful to her. As the oldest child, she would now have to assume the role of interim mamm to the younger kinner, once everything had been said and done. Then, she would have to face her growing years without the guidance and love of an adoring mother.

Still, it was Manuel who worried Faith the most. He didn't speak. He didn't eat. He barely had done much of anything since the undertaker had removed Rebecca's body to be prepared for the burial. When he finally returned Rebecca to the house later that evening, Manuel had barely glanced at the plain pine box that was carried into the house and set up in the cleaned out bedroom, the same room where, just hours before, she had died. The women had hurried into the room and dressed the body before permitting the beginning of what would be three days of viewing. During that time, over four hundred people would visit the Petersheim household, sitting for a while, passing by Rebecca's coffin, and expressing their condolences to Manuel, Rebecca's parents, and the children.

Faith had watched all of this in disbelief. *Surely this isn't happening*, she tried to convince herself. Truly she was dreaming and would awaken to find out that Rebecca was alive and well.

But it was indeed happening and she wasn't dreaming.

The day of the funeral, Faith had attended the service, sitting in the back with her parents as she listened to the strange words of the bishop, spoken in a language she had never bothered to learn, as he paced back and forth before the casket. It was open and Faith could see Rebecca, dressed in white, resting from within. She could barely take her eyes off the casket and only did so to glance at the children who sat solemnly next to Manuel in order of their respective ages: Anna, Gideon, Mary, Sadie, and Benjamin.

When the service was over, the people single-filed walked past the casket, pausing to briefly look, for a last time, at Rebecca. Faith was glad for her mother's steady hand on her arm as their turn came to say good-bye to Rebecca.

It was Rebecca's brother who had insisted that she'd ride in his buggy in the funeral procession following the service. In a daze, Faith had not argued, remembering all too well the last time that James had offered her a ride in the buggy on the evening when Rebecca went to her first singing. Faith had declined then but she didn't now. Instead, she crawled into the back of the buggy, seated next to two of his kinner, barely able to move, as James secured the front seat and helped his wife inside before climbing in behind her.

Only family and the closest friends were invited to the burial site so Faith's parents had parted before the members of the Petersheim and Yoder family left the house where the service was held. There were at least thirty buggies in the procession, the long line of grey topped buggies being pulled by black or chestnut horses following the wagon that carried Rebecca's coffin to her final resting place. Police blocked traffic at the intersections so that the buggies could progress in peace, not hindered by impatient drivers who might try to pass them impulsively and carelessly on the back roads.

At the cemetery, there had been one last viewing of the body before the undertaker shut the coffin and the men carried it over the grass and around the other gravestones to the hole that had been dug at the far end of the fenced-in plot of land reserved as the final resting place for the local Amish community. Faith followed the others toward the grave, shocked to see a mound of dirt and two shovels to the left side. She hadn't been to many funerals in her life but, from the few that she recalled, she had never seen loose dirt, just waiting to be tossed atop of the coffin.

A few words were said and the coffin was lowered into the hole. Faith cringed and looked away, hating the sound of the wood as it scraped the sides of the grave. Careful, she wanted to yell. That's my friend! The tears began again and she dabbed at her eyes with a wadded up tissue.

And then they began to fill in the grave.

Faith watched, speechless. No one moved. No one said a word. They just stared into the hole, watching as two men began to toss the dirt into it, the noise of the earth dropping onto the pine coffin echoing in the silence. Faith looked around at the mourners' faces, staring at their reactions, waiting for something, anything. But there was nothing. No expression of grief. No tears. No emotions. Just stunned faces watching as the mound of dirt began to transfer from the side of the grave onto the top of Rebecca's coffin.

A sob escaped Faith's mouth and she turned away. She couldn't watch this anymore. It was too morbid, too final. She started to walk away but she felt a hand on her arm, gently holding her back. She looked up and through her tears saw Manuel. He kept holding her arm, hindering her from leaving and, with a slight shake of his head, indicated that she should stay.

"It's her final journey, no?" he whispered sorrowfully.

"She would want us to stay." His eyes returned to the grave, watching as it gradually filled with the loose dirt. He sighed, a sad noise, and released Faith's arm.

No one spoke as they made their way back to the buggies. Faith walked slowly, her shoulders hunched over and her eyes downcast. She was wearing a long, plain black dress and the thought crossed her mind that under any other circumstances, Rebecca would have found this humorous, if not downright ironic. Indeed, if it were not for the lack of a prayer cap, her look and her demeanor were very similar to these of the Amish gathered at the funeral.

As the buggies pulled away from the cemetery, there was a hollow feeling in Faith's chest, as if she was abandoning Rebecca, leaving her in the cold, damp ground. She fought back another sob and covered her mouth with her hand, as if the pressure could keep her sorrow inside.

Back at the Petersheim's farmhouse, several of the Amish women from the church district had transformed the room that had been used for the funeral service into a dining room with two long tables, set for the meal. The older men and women sat at one table, men facing women. Faith did not know where to sit so she lingered by the door, watching all of this with a dazed expression on her face. No one seemed to notice her and, when she knew they were getting ready to pray, she slipped out the door, preferring to be by herself.

She walked toward the barn, trying to clear her head of the chaotic thoughts that raced through her mind. If only, she thought...If only we hadn't grown apart. If only I had stayed in closer contact. If only I had known that she was still trying to have more children. If only...

Yet, Faith knew that she could have twenty "if only's"

but not one of them made any sense. Rebecca had known, going into this pregnancy, that the doctors had warned her. Rebecca had played with her own life, taking her chances. And she had lost.

All for the love of a child that the mother would never meet, Faith realized. A child that, even now, was all but neglected, being watched by a neighbor woman, while the family mourned the loss of the mother.

Faith stood in the barn, breathing in the sweet scent of hay emanating from the square bales that someone had stacked against the wall. She could barely smell the cow manure, for it was a scent that she had grown immune to long ago, at her own father's farm. But there was something about hay that always put her in a better mood. It smelled like summer, fresh and clean. Full of the promise of renewal; of sustained life.

She reached out her hand and touched the bales, loving the prickly feeling of the hay on her skin. It reminded her of a time when she was younger, running barefoot through the Yoder's hayloft, taking turns with Rebecca on the rope swing that her daed had hung from the rafters. Sometimes, when they landed in the piles of loose hay, they would find big spiders in their clothing and the girls would scream, running out of the barn and looking for James or Aaron to brush off the scary looking creatures.

She smiled at the memory.

With a deep breath, Faith turned to leave the barn. She knew that she had to return to the house, face the relatives and share their grief. Yet, she dreaded it. She stood out among all of those Amish people. When they had been younger, the differences hadn't seemed so meaningful. Now, time had widened the gap in a way that was far too obvious to Faith. She wanted the day to end so that she could escape to her parents' farm, crawl into her bed, and try to forget the fact that Rebecca, her best friend, was permanently gone.

Quietly, she stole back into the house, avoiding the main room where the two tables were set. Instead, she went into the kitchen and stood at the counter, staring out the window. She looked at the view of the back paddocks and wondered how many times Rebecca had stood there, pausing from her chores to do just the same thing: watch and reflect.

"You need to eat, Faith," someone said at her elbow.

Faith glanced to her side to see Lydia, Manuel's sister, holding a plate of food. But she had no appetite. In fact, she hadn't for days. "No thank you," she managed to say.

"You'll get sick and what help will you be to Rebecca then?"

The question struck Faith as odd. What help *could she be* to Rebecca at all anyway? Rebecca was dead. Her husband would tend to the farm and her mamm would most likely move in for a while to help with the kinner. Surely one of the sisters would care for the infant. Faith had nothing left to give to the Yoder or Petersheim families.

"I reckon none, whether I eat or not," Faith retorted, immediately hating how sassy her words sounded.

Lydia gave a *tsk-tsk* with her tongue, clearly disapproving of what Faith had said as much as how she said it. "And I reckon she'd be right disappointed to hear you say something like that," Lydia said, her voice low. "I heard what her last request was. Her mamm told me. I know that her dying wish was not for you to starve yourself all together nor to turn your back on her family." Then, without another word, she thrust the plate at Faith and turned around, clearly done with the discussion.

Feeling rebuffed, Faith glanced at the plate in her hand and immediately felt sick to her stomach. She couldn't eat, not now. In fact, the way she felt at the present moment, she doubted she'd ever be able to find her appetite again. But she knew that Lydia was correct. Despite the lump in her throat and the pain in her stomach, she picked at the food, forcing a spoonful of the chow-chow and pickled beets into her mouth but avoiding the rest. Setting the plate on the counter, she turned and walked away, hating the way that she felt: angry and bitter for the loss of her friend, a friend that she had lost to both time and death.

It was Anna who approached her. Tall, willowy Anna with the big blue eyes that so resembled her father's. She wore a black dress and there were dark circles under her eyes. Like the others, there was no expression on her face. Blank. It was almost as if she was looking through Faith, not seeing her.

"May I talk to you, Faith?" she asked, her voice soft and flat.

"Oh Anna," Faith said, placing her hands on the girl's shoulders. "I'm so sorry."

Anna nodded her head twice but her expression never changed.

"How are you holding up?" It was the only thing that Faith could think to ask.

The girl shrugged. No response.

Faith wished that she could take back the question. What a stupid thing to ask, she scolded herself. How could any twelve-year old be holding up? Trying to salvage the exchange, Faith switched directions. "What did you want to talk about?"

"The baby," she said. "Who's going to take care of that baby?"

That baby. That still unnamed baby. That baby that somehow seemed to be getting the blame for everything, despite the fact that she was responsible for none of it. "Why, your aendis, I suppose."

Anna raised an eyebrow as if silently questioning Faith's answer.

"Why do you ask, Anna?"

"Summer's coming. That's busy time on the farm, ain't so? They have their own little ones to watch and farms to manage. I don't want to be stuck tending to that baby by myself," she said, her voice still soft and flat.

Careful, Faith warned herself. *This is dangerous ground.* "Your grossmammi will help out, too, Anna. You won't be alone," she said. "I am sure of that."

But Anna surprised Faith by disagreeing. "Nee," she admitted, shaking her head. "She's not well. And Daed's mamm died when I was younger."

"So what's really bothering you, Anna?"

"You'll come by and visit? Mayhaps even help a bit, ja?"

The question jarred Faith. Without Rebecca, what was the motivation? She hadn't been particularly close to the children. They had always been so quiet and reserved whenever Faith came around which, admittedly, had been less and less frequently. Of course, Anna was the oldest and Faith had a special relationship with her, having known her for the longest time, of all the Petersheim children. But, in all of her years, Anna had never truly sought out Faith. Now she was requesting that Faith would visit? Request Faith's help?

"Well I..." Faith simply didn't know how to respond.

"I..."

Anna frowned, obviously disappointed in Faith's response, or lack thereof. "You are my mamm's best friend, Faith. Mayhaps I need you," she admitted. "So that I can still know my mamm and feel her presence."

"Yes, Anna," Faith heard herself say. "Of course I'll come by and visit."

Satisfied, Anna nodded her head and, without another word, turned to walk back toward the other Amish people who, having finished their meal, were now standing around in small groups, offering words of comfort to Rebecca's husband, parents, children and siblings. Faith watched as Anna joined them, a small flock of people immediately turning their attention to her, the first-born child of the deceased.

For a few moments, Faith stood there, watching the transformation in Anna. Just a few days ago, she had been an innocent eleven-year old, wide-eyed and quiet, drinking in all that she could from her mamm. Today, she was the matriarch of the little Petersheim family. After the first few months, it would be Anna in charge of laundry and meals, sewing and gardening. Indeed, Faith realized, a heavy burden had befallen those slender eleven-year old shoulders. No wonder she wanted Faith to come by and help. She would need someone to lean on, to confide in.

Her eyes drifted to Manuel. He was standing among Rebecca's family, Gideon and Sadie by his side. Seven-year old Sadie was leaning against his leg, her head tipped forward as she stared at the ground. Gideon, at ten years of age, was trying to stand on his own as he grappled with his own feelings. But Faith could tell that he was struggling. A strong hand placed on his shoulder by his daed was enough to give the boy more strength. He stood a little taller and seemed to breathe easier, just knowing that his daed was nearby.

She had to leave. She couldn't stay there for one more minute. Yet, exiting was going to be a problem. She would have to interrupt the family, say her final condolences and goodbyes to Rebecca's parents, children, and husband. Anna's words rang in her ears and she knew that the promise she had made would have to be honored. She just didn't know when she would be able to do so.

"You are leaving, then?"

Manuel looked up when James said those words to Faith. His eyes tried to focus as he studied Faith's face.

"I best get going, yes," she affirmed.

"Nee," Manuel said firmly. "You should stay. We'll be alone soon, just the family. Rebecca would have wanted you to stay for a while."

Faith wanted to argue but the look in his eyes prompted her not to. Like Anna, there was a pleading tone to his voice, something unsaid but with a hidden need for Faith to be around. With a simple nod, she took a step back, her arm brushing against James' as she took her place among Rebecca's family.

It was after everyone else had left, with only Manuel and the children and Rebecca's immediately family remaining behind, that Faith realized her place among these people. She had known Rebecca for almost twenty-five years. Twenty-five long and mostly happy years. She had been friends with Rebecca, growing up alongside of her. She had spent nights at the Yoder's home, attended church services with Rebecca when they were younger, giggled into the night as they talked about other children, and ran across the pastures that separated their homes. Indeed, Rebecca had always considered Faith as part of the family. Only now, Faith realized, so did the rest of the people in the room.

Manuel stood up while the others sat around the living room. He crossed the floor and stopped before the large clock that hung on the wall. Faith hadn't realized that it was still idle, not working. When Manuel reached up, touching the hands and pushing them to point to the correct time, she remembered that the clock had been stopped when Rebecca had died. The others bowed their heads for a moment, quietly reflecting on what that moment meant. Time had stopped when Rebecca died but now, with the family looking on, Manuel was signaling that it was necessary for time to start again. Life was for the living, not to be left mourning the deceased. So the clock started to tick again.

Manuel returned to the circle of family, some sitting on the sofa and chairs in the kitchen while others had pulled up a bench to sit upon. He paused and placed his hand on James' shoulder, forcing a smile at his brother-in-law, before he took his seat on a folding chair next to Faith. He neither looked at her nor did he speak. But there was something calming about his presence beside her. Something both of them sensed, without communicating.

You take care of my children, Rebecca had said. *You help Manny.*

If only she knew how, Faith thought. In her world, she would feel comfortable talking to him. In her world, she would be able to console him. Yet, as much as Faith had grown up among these people, she knew very little about such matters. Her time had always been spent with Rebecca, giggling and laughing as young girls did. Aside from their close and friendly interaction as girls, teenagers then young women, there had been but little exploration of the actual culture in which Rebecca had been raised.

So when she excused herself to step outside, needing a breath of fresh air and a moment away from the suppressive heaviness of the room, she was surprised to see that Manuel had followed her. She was standing on the porch when she heard the door open. Glancing over her shoulder, she saw that it was Manuel and, immediately, she cast down her eyes.

"It's hard in there, ja?" he said softly, shoving his hands into his pockets. "I don't blame you for needing to get away."

She wasn't certain of how to respond. Instead of saying anything, she turned her head to look at the sky. The sun was setting behind the house and the sky before her was getting darker, taking its evening purple shade. The trees looked black and somber as the daylight faded away.

"It's hard to believe, isn't it?" She heard the words before she realized that she was the one who had actually expressed them.

"God called her home," he said. Despite the simplicity of the words, she could hear the sorrow in his voice. "It's not our place to question His reasons, Faith. I have to remind myself of that."

She looked at him, surprised at his confession. In all the years that she had known Manuel, he had never spoken so openly to her. Instead, she had always visited with Rebecca, spending her time with her friend and rarely any time interacting with Rebecca's husband.

"I came out here to tell you something," he offered, his voice gruff and low. He was staring at her, his blue eyes sad and watery. "I cannot thank you enough for what you did to help Rebecca. Not just now," he said. "But you were always there for her. And these past few days..." He hesitated, taking a deep breath. "Ja, vell, I just want you to know that you will always have friends and family here among us and among the Amish community, Faith."

His words surprised her. She had done no more or no less than she would have done for anyone else, perhaps less because she had felt intimidated around his family. The baby had certainly helped keep her busy as she had taken charge of tending to her while the others focused on the viewing and funeral arrangements until Rebecca's mamm took over the infant's care. "I don't know what to say to that, Manuel," she replied softly. "But I thank you for these words."

He nodded and backed up, reaching a hand behind himself for the door handle. Opening it, he started to turn as if to enter then, thinking twice, he looked back at Faith. "I know you're uncomfortable in there," he said. "You don't have to stay, Faith. You've done more than enough to honor Rebecca and help her family." He gave her a forced smile before he slipped through the door, hesitating just briefly to see if she intended to follow.

Taking a deep breath, Faith reached out her hand and placed it on the doorframe. She saw a look in his face, almost relief, when he realized that she was going to follow him back inside the house. Despite wanting to leave, wanting to put as much distance as she could between herself and the Petersheim farm and the memory of her best friend's death, she felt obligated to continue honoring Rebecca by doing the very thing that she had requested upon her deathbed...helping her best friend's family.

Chapter Three

It had been two months since Faith's last visit to the Petersheim's farm. With each passing weekend during that time period, a new wave of guilt overcame her. Yet, as more and more time separated her from the funeral, the harder it became to find a reason or the rationale to visit. However, when the school year had just ended, Faith knew she had no further excuses not to honor Anna's request. With ten weeks of summer stretched out before her, Faith talked herself into taking the ten-minute drive to Manuel's farm on the first Monday of her summer break.

The house appeared quiet. Despite the fact that the children were not outside playing, everything looked eerily the same. Laundry was hung on the line, drying in the warm summer sunshine. There were flowers planted around the porch, mostly pink and white, Rebecca's favorite colors. A fat cat lounged in the driveway, licking at its white paw before swiping at its ear. When her car pulled up to it, the cat lifted its head, stared defiantly at the vehicle, then lazily stood up, arched its back, and sauntered toward the barn.

Indeed, it was as if nothing had happened, as if time had continued without any recognition of what had occurred just two months ago.

Anna was the first one to greet her. Having just celebrated her birthday, the girl looked older than her twelve years, a plain white handkerchief covering her hair, tied primly under her chin. Her green dress was dirty and she had black circles under her eyes. But when she recognized Faith, she smiled and waved cheerfully.

A new wave of guilt washed over Faith. How could she have deserted Rebecca's children? Why had she waited so long to come visit?

"Oh Faith!" Anna gushed, rushing out to meet her in the driveway. "It's just right gut to see you!" In an unusual display of affection, Anna pressed her body against Faith's, hugging her lightly. She had lost weight, that was the first thing that Faith noticed. The second thing she noticed was how she clung to her, as if just needing that closeness with another woman, even if only for a few stolen seconds.

"I'm sorry it took me so long to stop by," Faith said, knowing how lame the words sounded when she said them. She felt guilty for having delayed in checking in on Rebecca's family. Every weekend, she had a different excuse. But none of them made up for the lost time that, she could see, had aged young Anna's face.

Anna didn't seem to notice. Instead, she pulled away and smiled up at Faith. "That's OK. You're here now."

Together, they walked toward the house.

"How is everyone doing?" Faith asked, not knowing how else to break the ice.

Anna glanced toward the barn. The expression on her face told Faith all that she needed to know. With a shrug, Anna turned back to look at Faith. "School's been out for a while so we're all pitching in to help."

It was a weak response and they both knew it.

"The baby?"

Anna took a deep breath and clucked her tongue, too much like her mother for Faith's taste. The child had aged, that was obvious. "Ruthie? She's finally sleeping through the nights," she admitted wearily. "Most nights, anyway."

"Who tends to her?"

Anna paused at the door and lowered her eyes. "Me now." She chewed on her lower lip. "Not going back to school in the fall. Teacher is coming here on Saturdays to work with me." She lifted her head. "I only have to get through the next two years. Bishop says if I can get to fourteen, I'll be just fine but Daed can't do it all by himself. He needs my help."

Without another word, she opened the door and passed through it. Faith followed, her heart in her throat at the thought that young Anna had to sacrifice her youth and her education in order to help the family. With so many aunts and cousins, certainly the Petersheims and Yoders could find a better solution? Still, Faith had always believed that the Amish took care of their own. If the teacher was willing to homeschool Anna, that was just what would be done. No questions, no complaints. Just compliance.

If the outside of the house looked the same, the inside, however, appeared completely different. For a moment, Faith could only stand in the kitchen doorway and look around at the disaster that greeted her. Dirty dishes in the sink. Toys scattered on the floor. A table covered with papers and plates. There were clothes on the sofa. Faith couldn't tell if these were dirty or clean. The floor needed to be swept. *No*, Faith corrected herself. *Washed and scrubbed and washed again.* Gone was the pristine kitchen from Rebecca's days with freshly waxed linoleum floors and shiny cherry cabinets. In its place was what Faith could only describe as a pigsty.

"What happened here?" Faith heard herself ask.

Anna exhaled and lifted up her hands, a gesture of defeat. "Can't do it all, I reckon."

No, indeed, Faith thought.

"Well," Faith finally said when she collected herself from the shock of seeing the house in such disarray. "Then I guess we best catch up with each other while tending to this kitchen. What do you say, Anna?"

It took almost three hours to clean up the mess that had greeted her. However, working alongside Anna had been the right thing to do. It gave them something to talk about as well as a purpose. It also created an opportunity to bond, to share thoughts and stories. When there was a lull in the conversation, Faith could ask her questions about where plates were stored or where the broom and cleaning supplies were kept. During that time, no one else came into the kitchen and the house remained silent. No noise. No laughter. No voices.

"Where is everyone?" Faith finally asked. "Where's the baby?"

Anna frowned as if trying to think of the correct answer. "Mary, Gideon, Sadie and Benjamin are helping daed with the mowing. Ruthie's still sleeping." She paused. "She sleeps a lot."

That didn't sound good. Faith dried her hands on a dishtowel and headed toward the stairs. "She's upstairs, I suppose? I want to check on her."

Slowly, she crept up the stairs, knowing that the baby would most likely be in Anna's room. Amish children shared rooms and if Anna was designated the primary caregiver to the infant that would be where she slept. On the second floor, everything was quiet. Too quiet. And dark. The shades were drawn, Faith suspected more so because no one bothered to open them rather than for the purpose of keeping the upstairs cool.

If the kitchen had been bad, the upstairs was worse.

Beds were not made. Clothes were not hung up. The second floor bathroom was filthy, a dark ring lining the bathtub. Shuddering, Faith opened doors until she found what she was looking for: the crib.

A small hand moved, waving in the air in a jerky motion. A noise, soft and sweet. Something in Faith's heart softened, forgetting her repulsion at the disarray of Rebecca's house, as she approached the side of the crib and peeked inside. Ruthie was laying on her blankets, her arms in the air and her eyes wide open. It was clear that she had not been sleeping. Yet, she had never cried for attention.

Reaching down to pick up the small baby, Faith felt overcome with grief at the way Ruthie responded to her touch. For a moment, the baby seemed surprised. Then, she cooed as Faith gently pressed the small body against her shoulder.

It was clear that Ruthie did not have a lot of attention. Just enough to survive. She wore fresh clothes and her diaper wasn't wet. But Faith suspected that most of her days were spent in the darkness of Anna's room while the twelve-year-old struggled to tend to the house chores.

"Come here, baby girl," Faith whispered softly, her hand rubbing the infant's back as she turned to leave the room. "Let's get you downstairs so you can enjoy the day."

Anna looked up when Faith entered the room, the baby Ruthie still pressed against her shoulder. She seemed surprised to see the baby, but she said nothing. "Best be getting the evening meal ready for the others," she mumbled, looking away.

The girl's reaction surprised Faith. Guilt? Resignation? Frowning, Faith carried the baby to the sofa, pushed the now folded clothing to the side and sat down. She stared down at

Ruthie, amazed at how pleasant the baby was. Her large blue eyes stared up at Faith and the hint of a smile played on her cherubic lips.

"She's grown so much," Faith said, trying to elicit a response from Anna.

"I reckon."

Faith examined the baby, seeing that the weaker leg, while not as crooked as the day she had been born, was still not as developed as the other one. "Has someone seen her about her leg?"

Anna shrugged, clearly not interested. "A doctor came to examine her and said it was twisted during birth. He reset it and she was in a cast for a while."

That was news. "Will she be able to walk? Did he say?"

Again, an uninterested shrug followed by a nod. "I reckon. Most likely with a limp, though. It's shorter than the other one."

Disappointed with the lack of interest that Anna had in her baby sister, Faith turned her attention to fussing over Ruthie. Clearly, the resentment was still lingering in the air. After all, it was Rebecca's love for Ruthie that had changed everyone's life. Rebecca had chosen Ruthie over the rest of them. "Well, I think she's beautiful," Faith gushed and took the infant's hands in her own, pleased to feel the baby grab them. "Looks like your mamm, don't you think?"

"I got to go downstairs," Anna said, avoiding Faith's question. "Be right back."

Faith watched as the girl disappeared down a doorway that led to the basement. She could hear Anna's footsteps on the wooden stairs as she descended. Standing alone in the kitchen, Faith looked down at the baby in her arms. *Rebecca's last gift*, she thought. Only it appeared that the gift was unappreciated.

When Anna emerged, she was carrying a jar of chow-chow and a jar of pickled beets. She walked over to the kitchen counter, making a broad sweep past Faith and Ruthie. With a bent head, she set about the task of preparing the evening meal. Faith watched, admiring how Anna moved about her chores with not one complaint, even though she was clearly weary.

"Is any of your mamm's family around to help?" Faith heard herself ask. Why would such a close-knit family not be there for the grandchildren? Why would they leave Anna to take on so much responsibility at such a tender age, she thought?

"Weekends, sometimes," Anna admitted, setting the plates at different spots on the table. She paused at the place where her mother used to sit and looked up at Faith. "You'll be staying for supper then?"

She didn't want to stay, didn't want to be around when the family would gather at that table to eat a meal without Rebecca to serve them. It didn't feel right to be in the house and to share supper with the family without Rebecca. "I don't want to intrude," Faith finally said.

"Nee," Anna insisted. "Daed will want to see you."

Feeling uncomfortable, Faith relented. It was the desperate look in Anna's eyes. Even if Faith could help with the baby while Anna prepared the meal, it was the least that she could do.

Shifting the baby in her arm, Faith sat down on the sofa and watched as Anna moved about the kitchen. She resembled Rebecca in her quick, short and precise movements, a solid purpose to each step. It dawned on Faith that, without much help in the house, Anna had taken on the role of mother to the others, quite a burden indeed at only twelve-years of age.

"How are you managing, Anna?" When Anna paused and looked over her shoulder at Faith, Faith tilted her head and peered back at the young girl. "I mean *really* managing, not the let's pretend everything is alright type of managing."

The girl exhaled loudly and leaned against the counter. "Oh Faith," she said, a sob escaping her lips. "I miss Mamm so much and no one will talk about her, no one speaks of her! It's almost as if she never existed and I just can't understand that."

Faith nodded. She had noticed that trend over the years. Those who died were rarely talked about among the Amish. When Rebecca's grandparents had died, life continued and the grossdaadihaus was cleaned out, neatly awaiting the years when new occupants would live there. "I miss her, too," Faith admitted, realizing for the first time how much that was true.

"What do you mean you're going away for two weeks?"

Faith stood in the creek, the cool water gently rushing over her toes. She didn't like the idea any more than Rebecca did. "I have to go," she said with a shrug of her shoulders. "My mother wants me to attend this sleep away Bible camp."

Rebecca's brow wrinkled as she frowned. "I never heard of such a thing! Sending your child away for two weeks!"

Faith was certain that Rebecca was telling the truth. After all, the Yoder family did everything together. It was very rare for any of them to be apart for more than one day. On a few very special occasions, Rebecca had slept over at Faith's house. More likely to happen, however, was Faith staying at Rebecca's.

That was what weekends and summer vacations were for, after all.

"What am I supposed to do for two whole weeks?" Rebecca was pouting. At twelve years old, she was feisty and sassy, still a tomboy in many ways. "That seems like a lousy summer vacation for you."

At this comment, Faith laughed. "Oh Rebecca," she said lightly. "At least I'll be studying the Bible!"

Clicking her tongue and rolling her eyes, Rebecca shook her head. "You can study the Bible at home or church. Don't need to go away for that."

Faith smiled, trying to lighten the mood. She hadn't wanted to tell Rebecca but she knew that she had to share the not-very-good news with her friend. Still, knowing that there was nothing to be done about it, Faith had decided to look on the bright side and try to be positive. "Mother says it will be fun. There will be lots of other Mennonite children there."

This comment did even less to appease Rebecca. Her eyes shot open, staring at Faith in horror. "You'll make new friends!" she gasped. "You might even find a new, bestest friend!"

And there it was, in all its glory. The truth. Not only would Rebecca miss Faith, but she was worried that Faith would come back with new friends, worldly friends, friends that would replace a simple Amish girl who couldn't compete with that world.

Standing before Rebecca, the water from the creek splashing on her ankles, Faith placed her hand on Rebecca's shoulder. "No one could ever replace you as my bestest friend," she said. "Never."

Something in Rebecca's expression softened. Her eyes, which had looked so fearful just seconds before, changed to *something different...the look of hope. "Never?"*

"Never ever, ever, Rebecca." And, in a rare moment of emotion, Rebecca let Faith reach out and hug her, a friendly hug that spoke of the bond between the young Amish girl and her Mennonite friend.

"Wie gehts?"

Faith looked up as she heard Manuel's voice. He walked into the kitchen, peering around the corner to see who was visiting. He must have noticed her car and, most likely, didn't recognize it as belonging to Faith. When he recognized the young woman sitting on the sofa and holding his infant daughter, Manuel stopped in his tracks, his eyes growing wide.

"Hello Manuel," Faith said, suddenly feeling awkward, as if she were invading his privacy. "I promised to stop by and visit with the children," she said quietly before quickly adding, "And you, of course."

"Ja, ja," he said, his eyes drifting around the kitchen. That, too, gave him a moment of pause as he noticed that, for the first time in a long while, there was cleanliness and order to his home. His hesitation was just long enough to display his discomfort. Clearly, without having to ask, he knew that Faith had seen the mess and been the one who helped Anna clean up. The color drained from his cheeks and he averted his eyes. "Right gut of you to do that," he said softly. But his reaction told her that he felt otherwise.

Taking a deep breath, Faith spoke her mind. "Manuel, it's going to take time to adjust. Everyone knows that."

He looked up at her, his blue eyes studying her face. As he did so, she had the opportunity to see that he looked tired and worn down. Two months must have felt like an eternity to him. "Ja vell," he said, reaching up to tug at the collar of his shirt. "Best be calling those kinner in for supper, then." He started to walk back to the door but, as he did, his eyes glanced over the table. Seven. Seven place settings were there. Just like when Rebecca was alive.

"Anna invited me to supper," Faith explained quickly. "I said no, I didn't want to impose. But she insisted and, that way, I can visit with the other children too."

He didn't respond, merely nodded his head, and walked back into the large washroom off to the side of the kitchen. Faith heard him open the screen door and call out in Pennsylvania Dutch for the other children to hurry into the house. A few moments later, they ran inside, as eager to greet Faith as Anna had been. Their enthusiasm for her visit did not go unnoticed by Manuel, too. He seemed to shrink away from them, watching his children clamor about the Englische woman, the smaller ones even climbing onto her lap, careful to not bump the baby.

They are starving, Faith thought. *Starving for the attention of an adult.* The thought made her feel even guiltier for having stayed away so long.

"Sadie!" Faith exclaimed. "I think you've grown two inches taller since I last saw you!"

Sadie grinned.

"What about me?" Benjamin demanded, puffing out his chest and trying to increase his height, a gleam in his eyes.

"Oh yes," Faith answered earnestly. "At least two inches! Maybe more."

Mary peered at Faith, her big brown eyes large and round. She was the most soft spoken amongst the children, the one that reminded Faith the most of Rebecca during her first years after becoming a baptized member of the Amish church, the *serious years* as Faith had called them, often teasing Rebecca after the fact. "We haven't seen much of you," Mary said, not unkindly. "It sure is right gut that you came."

Something pierced Faith's heart. Guilt. *Why did I stay away?* Seeing the children stand before her was a wonderful feeling, especially given their excitement at having Faith visit. And, in each child, she caught tiny glimpses of Rebecca. She wondered if Manuel saw that too and if those moments brought him joy or pain. Probably a combination of both, she pondered.

"Faith is staying for supper," Anna said. "So you two go wash up and sit down now."

Obediently, the children hurried to the sink and followed her instructions. There was no fighting, no pushing, no shoving. Faith smiled to herself, comparing their behavior to the children that she taught at school. Despite being cousins in religion, Mennonite children were certainly not as well behaved as Manuel and Rebecca's. That spoke well of how Rebecca and her husband had raised them. But it gave Faith reason to pause as she looked down at the baby in her arms. Without Rebecca, how would Ruthie fare?

Once everyone was seated at the table, Manuel bent his head and the children did the same. During the silent prayer, Faith couldn't help but steal glances at each of the children. It felt awkward sitting at the supper table without Rebecca seated opposite Manuel. Instead, that spot was openly vacant, a visual reminder of their mother's permanent absence.

Manuel gently cleared his throat and lifted his head. His eyes traveled around the table, pausing briefly at Anna and he tried to smile. "A right gut job you have done, dochder," he said. "Again."

His praise pleased the young girl. "Faith wanted to help but I insisted that she was here to visit, not help with kitchen work," Anna said gaily.

"I wouldn't have minded," Faith replied, taking the bowl of pickled beets that Sadie passed to her. "But you certainly seem to have inherited your mamm's love of the kitchen."

Silence.

Faith wasn't surprised. She knew that, within the Amish community, deceased members of the family weren't discussed, not openly. She hadn't expected a reaction from the kinner or Manuel. Still, Faith wasn't going to ignore the large white elephant in the room. "I was surprised, Manuel," she started, staring directly at him. "At how much responsibility Anna has taken on, although I must say that she's doing a wonderful job, handling it all."

His blue eyes seemed to grow distant, as if a cloud passed over them.

Faith took his continued silence as permission to continue. "I'm surprised Rebecca's mamm isn't here," she ventured, wondering at what point she would be crossing that unspoken line in the sand.

To her surprise, it was Anna who responded. "Grossmammi hasn't been well, Faith."

This was news indeed. Vaguely, Faith recalled Anna mentioning something about Rebecca's mamm at the funeral. But Rebecca's mamm had looked healthy enough. At the time, Faith had interpreted Anna's comment to reference her emotional state at the loss of her daughter, not her physical well-being. "Is she alright, what is wrong?" Faith asked, alarmed at the news. Another wave of guilt washed over her. She had yet to visit the Yoder's since Rebecca's death.

"They think it's the cancer," Manuel stated, his voice emotionless. "But she won't get treatment. Not from doctors anyway."

Faith frowned. "They *think* it's cancer?" In her world, it either *was or wasn't* cancer. There wasn't any *thinking* about it.

"In the spine," he said. "She's in a lot of pain, losing weight, and always tired. But won't go to the doctors."

Like mother, like daughter, Faith thought to herself. Growing up, she knew that some Amish scorned modern medicine, preferring a more holistic approach to managing health issues. Clearly the Yoder's were on that side of the fence.

"Well, I'm sorry to hear that," was all Faith could think of as a reply.

But the news about Rebecca's mamm certainly explained a lot. The rest of the Yoder daughters were married with their own small children, some of them living faraway, and the men working the farms, there wasn't anyone else on the Yoder side of the family to assist during this time of need.

The rest of the meal passed by with more awkward silence. This time, Faith let it linger, her mind in a whirlwind over what she had experienced that day.

Never had she imagined that one single event could so dramatically change the course of life for so many. She watched the children, her heart breaking with each long, drawn out silent moment. With summer having arrived, the children were no longer in school and that meant a long, hard few months for all of them. Suddenly, her own enthusiasm for having time to herself until September vanished. With a sigh, she pushed back her plate. Finishing the food was not an option now, not with the knot that had just developed in her stomach.

Chapter Four

It hadn't taken very long for Faith to make up her mind. When she had left the Petersheim farm, she felt as if she were in a trance. It had stunned her, the level of grief that Rebecca's family was feeling as well as the need for healing. They were lost, like sheep in a field that wandered too far from the flock. Just as Jesus prayed for the one lost sheep, Faith had spent the weekend praying for her six lost ones. Seven, if she counted Ruthie.

On Saturday, she hadn't been able to focus on her chores. Her parents noticed how pensive and quiet she was. Yet, she hadn't shared with them the experiences of her visit. Instead, she had been reflecting on the events, ideas fermenting, trying to come up with a solution.

No, it hadn't taken long to decide. Perhaps she had known it from the moment she left the farm after that supper. Indeed, she knew what she had to do.

It was Sunday after church when she approached her parents, sharing with them the events that had transpired during her visit and the promise that she had made Rebecca so many years ago after Rebecca's miscarriage. She paced the floor as she talked, shaking her head as she recalled the look in Anna's eyes and the quiet baby that stayed confined to her crib most of the day.

They were supportive. "It's the Christian thing to do," her mother had agreed. That had helped tremendously. The fact that her parents understood the dilemma and Faith's need to help. After all, Faith had explained, it was the only way that she could sleep at night, at peace with herself, knowing that Rebecca's family had some help, a mother figure to guide them or, at least, to get them back on track.

So, at seven in the morning on Monday, Faith found herself standing on the front porch of the Petersheim's house, her heart racing and her knees feeling weak as she waited for someone to answer the door.

"What on earth...?" Manuel had said when he opened the door, genuinely surprised to see Faith standing there.

Taking a deep breath, Faith didn't wait for an invitation as she entered the house and set her purse on the floor by the door. "Manuel," she started, hoping that her inner strength held up for what she had to say. Leveling her gaze at him, she announced her intention before her false bravado dissipated. "I'm here to help your family and I won't take no for an answer!"

He stared at her, his eyes still trying to make sense of what he saw before him. Despite having been up for hours already, he looked tired and drained.

"Your children need someone here to help them, especially Anna and little Ruthie," Faith continued. "Rebecca would be ashamed of how this house looked last week. It's too much for Anna to do this alone."

He lowered his eyes, embarrassed. "I reckon," he said.

His response did not appease her. Instead, she found herself angry. "Then why haven't you done anything? Why haven't you hired someone to help? If Rebecca's family couldn't help, what about yours?"

"People helped in the beginning," he said softly. "But I didn't think..."

Faith shook her head, cutting him off. "No, you didn't."

She paused, looking around the kitchen. Already it was a disaster, despite her hard efforts just three days earlier. "I'm going to make it up to Rebecca. I'm going to help while I'm on summer break. Take care of her family, her house, and that very special little baby that seems to be too much of a burden to be loved properly."

Manuel's eyes narrowed and he glared at her. "That ain't so!"

She lifted an eyebrow as she met his fierce look, saddened that her words had struck a chord within him. That only spoke to the truth of what she had just said. "Oh? When was the last time you held that baby?" When he looked away, refusing to meet her eyes, she merely shook her head. "I thought so."

Without another word, Faith swept into the kitchen and immediately began opening cabinets in order to set the table for breakfast. "I'm trusting no one has eaten yet?"

"Nee," he admitted softly.

"Good. That will be the first order of business. Breakfast at seven-thirty." With that, she hurried to the refrigerator and opened the door, quickly assessing what was inside. There wasn't much. No sausage, no fresh bread. But she found enough eggs to allow for a large pan of scrambled eggs. And the pantry had rolled oats. That would suffice, she thought. Eggs and oatmeal before a late morning trip to the food store to replenish the supplies and prepare a proper noon meal.

Within minutes, the fragrant smell of sizzling eggs filled the kitchen and she heard the pounding sound of bare feet hurrying down the stairs. Glancing over her shoulder, Faith smiled as she greeted the round face that stared at her through the banister.

"Good morning!" she sang cheerfully, despite wishing she were still curled up under the covers of her own bed. "Best get down here and set that table, dear Sadie. Still needs some silverware and glasses."

Sadie rubbed her eyes and blinked, her hair hanging down her back in an unkempt tangle of curls. "What are you doing here?" she asked, a yawn escaping her lips.

"Early bird gets the worm," Faith answered cheerfully. "And I bet your daed sure could use a big meal after getting up so early for the morning milking." She gestured to Sadie. "Come on," she encouraged. "Help me with the table."

"Where's Anna?" Sadie asked, sliding down the rest of the stairs before padding across the floor, her bare feet making a soft noise against the linoleum.

"Not certain," Faith admitted. "Your daed was just here but he went back to the barn, I suppose."

Sadie pursed her lips and looked around. "She's probably with that baby."

That baby. Not Ruthie. Not the baby. But *that* baby. "You mean sweet little Ruthie?" Faith asked. "Such a precious little one."

A simple shrug from Sadie.

"You don't think so?"

"She doesn't do much," Sadie admitted, making a face, which caused Faith to laugh.

"Well, she's just a baby," Faith said. "You'll have more fun with her when she's a little older and can move around."

"Maybe," Sadie responded but didn't sound convinced.

The table was set and the food was displayed in the center of it when the door opened and Manuel walked in. He eyed the table with a hurt look in his eyes and, once again, refused to look directly at Faith. At the same time, Anna, Mary, and Gideon came downstairs, a look of confusion on their faces as they saw Faith waiting patiently for them to take a seat at the table. Their eyes noticed the set table and their noses smelled the food. There was a moment, just a flicker of understanding and Faith saw Anna smile, a look of relief and joy spreading across her face.

"Where are Benjamin and Ruthie?" Faith asked Anna.

"Upstairs still. Sleeping."

Faith shook her head. That just wouldn't do. "I'd appreciate it if you went up and brought down the baby, please. And wake Benjamin to join us. We have a lot to do today."

Obediently, Anna turned and walked back upstairs, returning momentarily with Ruthie in her arms and, a few second later, a still sleepy Benjamin in tow. He rubbed at his eyes as he looked around the kitchen. His suspenders hung down by his waist and his shirt was not tucked in. But, when he saw the table set and smelled the food, he smiled at Faith, a big grin that exposed a lost tooth in the front.

"A breakfast? A real breakfast?"

The delight in his voice at something so simple as a home-cooked meal to start the day broke her heart. How could so much have gone wrong in such a short period of time?

"Let's get you straightened up, Benjamin. Make you look handsome for the meal," she said lightly and hurried over to help him tuck in his shirt and slip his suspenders over his shoulders. "There! Like a proper young man."

He beamed at the compliment and scurried over to the table.

The entire time, she was aware that Manuel was

watching her, his finger rubbing at his chin and a concerned look on his face.

"Let's sit everyone for the blessing," Faith instructed, not knowing where her strength and determination were coming from. *For Rebecca,* she told herself. *It's only for Rebecca. She wanted me to do this.*

After the silent blessing over the meal, no one talked but the children immediately dove into the food. Eggs were passed around and the younger kinner devoured the oatmeal, sprinkling brown sugar over the top. Manuel picked at the food, barely eating anything. He did, however, drink down the coffee that Faith had placed in front of him. When she saw that his cup was empty, she stood up and hurried over to the stove to pour him some more. He thanked her, his eyes still downcast as he reached for the coffee mug.

"Your mamm was my oldest and best friend," Faith said when everyone was scraping the remains of their breakfast from their plates. "She would be very unhappy to see what is happening here."

"Faith," Manuel started slowly, shaking his head. The one word, her name, was a warning, an indication that she should stop. She was crossing an invisible line.

Holding up her hand, Faith stopped him. "I owe it to her," Faith said. "I owe it to my friend to help out for a while. I'm fortunate enough that I can."

A look of relief swept over Anna, a look that did not go unnoticed by Faith.

"And don't say that you don't need my help," Faith added. "I'm sorry, Manuel. But you do."

He didn't argue with her. How could he, when he knew what she had faced during the previous visit? The mess in the kitchen. The upstairs in disarray. The children quiet and depressed.

"It's just hard," he admitted softly. "I miss her..."

Faith glanced at the faces of the children, shifting Ruthie in her arms. "I'm sure you do. All of you. And so do I. But it's time to get back to living. Your mamm wouldn't have wanted you to die alongside her." She paused, but not long enough to permit them to comment. "Here are my thoughts for the day," she began. "I'd like to take a look at that garden your mamm planted. I'm sure it needs some tending to, weeding and watering to start." She turned to look at Manuel. For a moment, he stared at her. His expression was blank. She couldn't read what he was thinking. Had she crossed a line? "But only if you can spare the help," she added.

Silence.

"And then I will drive to the market, replenish the food pantry. You seem low on a lot," she said quietly, waiting for a reaction, *any* reaction, from Manuel.

It took a few, long seconds for him to gather his thoughts. She watched as he seemed to be trying to figure out how to respond properly. It was clear that he was conflicted by her offer. And then it came,

"You don't need to do this," he finally said.

"I think I do," Faith replied gently. "No one else is doing it and I see a great need here."

And that was the big question that kept lingering in her mind. *Why was no one else helping?* All of her life, she had lived alongside the Amish. She believed she had learned a lot about their ways: their culture, their religion, their lifestyle. She wondered where the extended family was in Manuel's time of need. It was unlike the community to not step up and help out.

Manuel cleared his throat and met her questioning eyes. "People visit on Saturdays," he said. "They bring food then."

But what about the rest of the week, she wanted to ask.

"Well, I'm here *now* to help," Faith proclaimed.

Without being asked, Anna stood up and began to clear the plates from the table. Her sister, Mary, quietly followed her older sister's example while Sadie leaned her head against her hand and watched Faith. There was something about Sadie, Faith thought, that reminded her of Rebecca in her youth. She was feisty and electric, curious and determined. Mary, on the other hand, was more like Rebecca during her final years: quiet and soft, a mature woman before her time. And Anna was somewhere in-between. It was interesting to get to know Rebecca's children and, for the first time, she regretted not having taken the time to do so when Rebecca was still alive.

Manuel pushed his chair back from the table and stood up, his tall frame filling the space at the end of the table. He glanced at Gideon and Benjamin then gestured toward the door. "Best start cleaning the dairy," he said softly. As if on cue, the boys jumped up and hurried to the door, grabbing their straw hats from the bench and dashing outside. Manuel paused, turning to look at Faith one last time.

"I'll accept your help for today," he finally said. "But we'll talk privately about this later." His eyes traveled momentarily toward Sadie then swept across the room to where the other two girls were beginning to wash the plates. "Can't agree to this, Faith. Just ain't right." Without another word, he headed toward the door, his shoulders hunched over and his hands thrust into his pockets.

He was defeated, that much was clear. Faith saw it in his demeanor. Quiet, reserved, barely able to take charge. Where was the Manuel from the past? The Manuel who had always been the strong one, the happy one, the one that could be leaned upon for support? Where was his faith, she wondered? That all-powerful Amish faith in God and God's will? Shaking her head, she tried to push away the questions, knowing that there were simply no answers. It had, after all, only been two months since Rebecca passed away. Only time would heal the wounds of the family's heart. She just hoped that she had enough time to heal her own.

Faith was crying. She couldn't understand why God would do this to her family. Over and over and over again. Why did God give her mother such longing for children only to keep taking away any hope? Her mother had just lost another baby, this time in the fifth month. It had been a surprise pregnancy. Faith was almost twelve. But the joy of a new life, a small baby brother or sister, had truly excited everyone.

And then it was gone.

For her mother, the loss was devastating. She had always had such trouble conceiving and her only successful pregnancy had been Faith. While her parents had smothered her with love and affection, Faith knew that her father would have loved a boy, a son to whom he could pass down the farm. When the pregnancy had progressed into the second trimester, everyone thought that this was going to be it: the sibling for Faith and, God willing, the son for her father.

"Oh, you will love having a baby in the house!" Rebecca had gushed when she had initially heard the news of Faith's mother's pregnancy. "It's so wonderful to watch them grow and to love them!"

Coming from Rebecca, that was expert advice. There was

always a baby at the Yoder farm. Rebecca's older sisters always seemed to have a baby in tow. Plus, her one brother lived next door in the grossdaadihaus with his wife and their newborn son.

Indeed, the loss of the baby, a boy at that, had hit everyone in the family individually. For Faith, she knew that was her last chance of having a brother or sister. For her mother, it was the end of her ability to conceive. And for her father, it was the loss of a dream...the dream of a son to teach the wonderful art of farming and to shape into a miniature mold of himself.

"We get to ride in your car?" Benjamin's eyes were wide open and he could hardly contain his grin.

Faith laughed. His curiosity reminded her of Rebecca. "Oh Benjamin! Have you never ridden in a car then?"

"Nee," he said. "Daed drives a horse and buggy."

Sadie puffed up her chest. Ever the big sister, Faith thought. "It's just like riding in a horse and buggy, only faster."

Mary gave her sister the familiar *tsk tsk*, so reminiscent of Rebecca and Rebecca's mamm. "As if *you* have ridden in a car before, sister."

"Now, now," Faith said calmly. She switched into teacher mode with the children. "Sadie happens to be correct. It is faster than a horse and buggy." She leaned down to Benjamin. "And you don't get the horse hair floating through the open window into your mouth!" He giggled at that statement. Faith smiled and stood up again. "I'm happy to take any of you for a car ride. I reckon that we will have plenty of time for that over the summer, don't you think?"

Sadie and Benjamin bobbed their heads in serious agreement while Anna looked on, smiling.

"For today," Faith continued. "I need Sadie and Benjamin's help at the store. Anna, perhaps you might care to ride along too while Mary watches Ruthie? You'll know what your mamm would normally stock in the house to cook for your daed and the kinner, and that would help."

"What about Gid?"

Benjamin's question startled Faith. She looked around the room, not seeing Gideon anywhere. She hadn't forgotten him. But he had disappeared with Manuel after breakfast. "Isn't he helping your daed?"

Benjamin nodded.

She spared him a smile. "It's truly good that you thought of your brother, Benjamin. But I think he's of more help to your daed than to me, don't you agree?"

At the Smart Shopper on Route 23, Faith parked her car and waited for the children to get out. Benjamin had a difficult time unbuckling his seat belt and Faith quickly hurried to help him. She showed him how to press the red button and smiled at his amazement over the simple device.

No one seemed to pay any attention to the three Amish youth who accompanied the clearly non-Amish woman. Despite wearing a simple pastel dress and flat shoes, Faith looked like a typical Englischer. Growing up, she had never taken to wearing a typical Mennonite head covering, although her mother wore one at church.

Sadie and Benjamin took turns pushing the shopping cart down the wide aisles as Anna helped direct Faith as to what to purchase. Canned goods, flour, sugar, fresh meat, and vegetables. By the time they were finished, Faith had to help Benjamin and Sadie navigate the heavy cart.

"Oh my," Faith said as she assessed the conveyer belt.

"That's an awful lot of food!" She glanced at Benjamin. "Do you think we'll ever eat it all?"

"That depends if you are a good cook!" he replied and Sadie nudged him with her elbow. Startled, he looked at his sister and frowned. "Well it's the truth!"

Faith laughed and tousled his brown, loopy curls. "You let me know after we cook a nice dinner today, OK?"

Benjamin had grinned, that lopsided smile, and nodded his head. "I can do that, Faith!" Like Gideon, Benjamin favored Manuel in appearance over Rebecca. Faith could imagine Manuel as a child whenever she looked at Benjamin: curly brown hair, bright blue eyes, and a charm about him that exuded goodness. But his personality was much more like Rebecca, the Rebecca of Faith's youth. Gideon, however, was Manuel through and through in both appearance and temperament.

By the time they made it back to the farm, the mood of the children was joyful, with teasing and laughter filling the car. No one complained about having to carry in the shopping bags or about helping Faith figure out where to store their supplies in the kitchen. Immediately after everything was put to order, Faith glanced at the clock and noticed that it was almost ten-thirty. She needed to start cooking the mid-day meal.

"Best get started peeling those potatoes," she urged Sadie and Mary.

"What shall I do?" Anna asked.

Faith glanced around the kitchen, noticing that there were toys and papers scattered around the sitting area. "Perhaps you could tidy up over there, Anna; makes it nice for your daed to come home to an orderly house. Benjamin, would you sweep the floor a bit?"

"Aw, that's girls work!" he groaned in response.

Fighting a smile, Faith knelt down before him and leaned toward his ear. "If you do, I think I could be convinced to make some chocolate chip cookies later this afternoon."

With that, he stood up straight, a serious look on his face. "Sweeping the floor, then. I'm right on it, Faith," he announced and hurried to the washroom to get the broom, leaving Faith laughing at his newfound spark of enthusiasm for helping in the kitchen.

By the time Manuel and Gideon walked into the house, there was order in the kitchen with a table that had been set by the girls and the good smell of cooked chicken and mashed potatoes filling the room. Faith was standing at the sink, washing some pans when she heard the washroom door open. She turned off the water, shaking her hands dry as she turned around, apprehensive over Manuel's reaction when he entered the room.

He stood in the doorway for a moment, his eyes scanning the room and seeing everything through fresh eyes. When he noticed the table, set with a simple tablecloth and steaming food, he lifted his eyes and sought out Faith's. There was something about his expression, a mixture of emotions. She thought he looked sorrowful as well as relieved. Yet, like most Amish men, his nature was to not speak of such feelings. Instead, he merely nodded his head once as he entered the room.

He crossed the room toward the sink and hesitated as Faith stepped back so that he could wash his hands. She handed him a dishtowel when he was finished and noticed that he hesitated before taking it. "Danke, Faith," he said, his voice low as he dried his hands.

Unlike the previous visit, there was more animation around the kitchen table. Faith sat on the bench next to Sadie and Mary, listening to the conversation between Benjamin and Gideon about the field work that had been done earlier. She could see disappointment in Benjamin's face about having missed out on time spent outdoors and she took the opportunity to speak up.

"Perhaps, Benjamin, you might help your daed this afternoon," she suggested. "The girls and I are going to tackle some of the gardening."

Benjamin beamed and turned toward his father. "Could I, Daed?"

Manuel glanced at Faith, his forehead wrinkled in disapproval. Immediately, she knew that she may have crossed a line by speaking up yet again. At the same time, she didn't care. These children were starving for normalcy in their life and it meant that Manuel had to step up and take the boys, both boys, under his wing once again. "I reckon," he mumbled, still looking at Faith.

Ignoring his disapproving look, Faith turned to Anna. "I think we need to do some weeding this afternoon. What do you think, Anna? Flower beds? The garden? I noticed your mamm's garden looks more like a jungle for monkeys than a place to grow food for people!"

Sadie and Benjamin giggled.

"And those flower beds!" She teased. "We need to keep up your mamm's reputation for having the most beautiful and creative flower beds in the g'may!"

Anna nodded. "I agree."

Faith smiled. "So, outside work for us all this afternoon!"

Benjamin frowned, a pout on his face when he heard her proclamation. "What about my chocolate chip cookies?"

Everyone laughed and Faith thought she even saw a hint of a smile on Manuel's face. *This is good*, she told herself. *Slowly but surely, it will happen.*

"And, of course, chocolate chip cookies for everyone!"

After the dinner meal was over, Faith stood at the kitchen sink, washing the dishes as the girls brought them over from the table. Anna took charge of putting away the left overs and Sadie wiped down the table, all without being asked. Mary stood beside Faith, a dishtowel in her hand to wipe dry the wet dishes before stacking them on the counter. As she finished with the last plate, Faith turned off the water faucet and glanced out the window. She could see Benjamin skipping along behind his older brother, a newfound energy to his step. It pleased her to see that, with a little direction, the family was willing to respond, all but Manuel who seemed more than uncomfortable with her presence around the house.

I'm doing this for Rebecca, she reminded herself. *Not Manuel.*

Outside, Faith let the younger girls guide her to the garden where she quickly assessed that it was in dire need of attention if they were going to produce any vegetables that summer. "Oh help," she said as she saw the overgrown mass of weeds. "Looks like we have our hands full, don't we?"

They spent the next hour working their way through the rows, plucking anything green that looked unidentifiable. While Mary was quiet as she worked, Sadie was just the opposite. She was full of constant chatter, sharing stories with anyone who would listen and asking questions of Faith about teaching the Englische children.

"Your school sounds a lot different than ours," Sadie said, an incredulous look on her face as if she couldn't fathom any other type of school than the one-room schoolhouse she attended. "No German? No hymn singing?"

Faith shook her head. "No German and the only singing the students do is with their music class, although they sure enjoy hosting a winter and spring concert for their parents."

Sadie grinned. "We do that! Only this past spring..." Her voice trailed off and she looked down at the pile of weeds at her feet. For a moment, Faith thought that she might start to cry, clearly thinking of her mamm's passing which most likely resulted in the children missing the spring concert. But, with a deep breath, Sadie returned to the task at hand. "Well, mayhaps next year."

Reaching out, Faith touched Sadie's shoulder. "I bet I could come to your winter concert next year," she said. "Although summer has only just started and, rather than think of something so far away, I'd much prefer to enjoy the glorious weather, wouldn't you?"

Appeased, Sadie nodded her head and went back to work.

"Faith," Anna called from the edge of the porch. "Ruthie's awake."

Wiping her hands on the bottom part of her dress, Faith glanced at Mary and Sadie. "Guess that's my call," she said lightly. "If you get too hot, come inside. I'll make some lemonade for everyone after I get Ruthie situated."

It was almost three before the girls could be heard clamoring up the porch steps, Sadie chattering away about something that two girls had said the previous day at church. She was still talking when Anna and Mary both stopped walking, standing just inside the doorway and staring at the kitchen. Ruthie was lying on her back in the middle of a soft blanket on the floor while Faith worked. The table was already set for supper, a plate and utensils at each place setting. In the center of the table, Faith had placed a small glass filled with purple lilacs that she had snuck from the lilac bush that was located just beyond the kitchen's side door.

"You're back already!" she exclaimed, smiling as she motioned for them to wash their hands. "I bet everything looks right as rain out there in those gardens!"

"You made supper?" Anna asked, her mouth still hanging open.

"Well, of course," Faith responded. "You were busy working outside. I'm sure all of your brothers and your daed will appreciate an early supper after having worked so hard today. Speaking of which," she added, hurrying to the counter where she had a large plastic pitcher with a stack of cups ready for refreshments. "I made a pitcher of lemonade and thought that we should take it out to those boys. Field work is sure to make them thirsty."

Mary sniffed the air. "Do I smell cookies?"

Faith looked surprised at her question. "Well of course! I promised your brother, didn't I? I have them in that Tupperware over there, if you wouldn't mind taking that. I can carry Ruthie if Anna will take the lemonade." Within minutes, they were back outside and headed across the driveway and toward the backfield where Faith had last seen Manuel and his sons.

Careful not to step on the growing rows of corn plants, they navigated the field until they came to the top of the hill where Manuel was repairing a fence that a tree limb had taken down during the previous week's storm. When Benjamin noticed the approaching girls, he let out a whoop which made both Gideon and Manuel jump.

Leaning back on his heels, Manuel lifted his hand to his forehead, blocking the sun as he peered at the approaching figures. He watched, not moving for a few minutes until they were closer. Then, setting the hammer on the ground, he stood, pausing to stretch out the kinks in his back from having knelt for so long. "What's this?" he asked.

"Refreshments," Faith answered.

"A picnic!" Sadie shouted happily at the same time.

"Picnic?" he repeated, lifting his hat from his head and wiping the bead of sweat from his brow. Faith noticed that his curly hair was flattened on the top, where the hat had just rested. "Ja vell, that sure was a right gut idea," he finally said. "It's hot working out here in the sun." He glanced at the sky. "Reckon it will be a hot summer, then."

"Here Daed," Anna said.

Manuel took the glass of lemonade that Anna poured for him. "Danke, dochder," he said, forcing a smile before he lifted it to his lips. Mary opened the Tupperware container and offered it to her father. "And cookies?" He looked up at Faith, a mixture of concern and appreciation in his face. "You have been busy, ja?"

She shifted Ruthie in her arms. "Many hands…" she started to say lightly.

"…make light the work!" Sadie and Benjamin finished the sentence for her in unison.

"That it does," he said softly, a sigh escaping his lips. "Best not be getting used to such treats, kinner. Faith has her own things to do and can't be coming every day."

At this, Faith raised an eyebrow. "Why ever not? It's my intention, Manuel, like I said over dinner, to be here for these children...your children...during the summer. Unless you have someone else to help, I see no reason to turn me away."

"Daed?" Anna started to plead, but one stern look from her father caused her to immediately lower her eyes and remain silent on the subject. It was clear that she was too aware that, if Faith did not return, the burden of the household duties would fall back on her shoulders.

Finishing his lemonade, Manuel handed the cup back to his daughter and nodded at Faith. "Danke" was all he said before he knelt down and picked up the hammer and returned his attention to fixing the fence.

She knew he wasn't pleased with her intentions but she couldn't understand why. With Rebecca's mamm being ill and his own mamm having passed away years before, there were but few options available to the Petersheim family. Still, she wasn't about to worry about his reaction. Once again, she reminded herself that she was doing this for Rebecca and the children, not Manuel. He had his hands full dealing with the farm work and eventually would see that her solution, even if temporary, was the only one available to him and the kinner.

Chapter Five

Faith stood by the edge of the garden, Rebecca's garden, her hands on her hips and a satisfied look on her face. In just two weeks, it had been transformed from an overgrown cluster of weeds that were choking the fledgling vegetables to a beautiful plot of land with green plants that boasted of tiny flowering buds on the tomato stalks, beans hanging from the vines, and the hint of zucchini and squash. A plump bumblebee buzzed by, landing on one of the tomato stalks before flying away toward the barn.

With the help of Mary and Sadie, there were no weeds left in the garden. After two days of clearing the soil, they were now on a maintenance routine. Faith had made a game out of it, letting the girl with the largest bucket of weeds select the type of cookies that she'd make for them in the afternoon. More often than not, it was young Sadie who won. Her energy was boundless as was her love of sugar drop cookies.

With a daily routine and positive encouragement, Faith had noticed a significant change in the household. Anna seemed more relaxed and less stressed about little things. The bags under her eyes had begun to disappear and she was even taking an interest in Ruthie. The more attention Faith bestowed on the baby, the more the rest of the children started to warm up to their youngest sister. Even the boys seemed re-energized by Faith's presence in the home.

The only one who seemed distant and withdrawn was Manuel. He was pleasant enough, for sure Faith certainly couldn't fault him for that. His manners were impeccable and he was more than polite. But, ever since that first day when Faith had showed up at the farm, barging into their lives without so much as asking permission, he hadn't had much to say. In fact, he seemed to be avoiding her.

Oh, there had been that one conversation, the one when she had left that first day. He had waited in the barn until it was time for Faith to leave. It was half past five and she had to return home, spend some time thinking about the day and decompressing.

Besides having prepared a light supper for the family, Faith had made certain that baby Ruthie had been fed, washed, and readied for bed before bidding the children good-night. To her relief and surprise, Anna had walked her to the door and given her a big hug, thanking her and making her promise that she would come back the next morning. When Faith had pulled away, she was even more surprised to see tears in Anna's eyes. What a burden, she realized, for a young lady barely on the brink of womanhood to confront!

Her mind was in a whirl. So, as she sat in her car, staring ahead at nothing, she barely noticed that Manuel was suddenly standing on the other side of her car, his hands on the open window as he knelt down and peered inside.

"You scared me!" she had exclaimed, jumping when she finally noticed him.

"Didn't mean to," he had replied earnestly. Then, he had glanced over his shoulder at the house, making certain that none of the children were outside and able to overhear the conversation. Satisfied that the kinner were back inside, he turned his attention back to Faith. "It's not necessary to come here, Faith," he had said slowly. "I appreciate your help today but we have to learn to manage on our own, ja?"

Faith had frowned at his words. That was his rationale? He certainly hadn't demonstrated the ability to manage so far. "I disagree, Manuel."

"Disagree?"

A foreign concept, Faith had realized, for an Amish man. After all, Amish women were taught that the head of the household was the husband. Disagreeing with the husband didn't come with that territory. She was quite certain Rebecca hadn't expressed disagreement with Manuel too often, if at all, during their marriage.

"Yes, I disagree. Anna is too young to take on this responsibility and the other children need someone to help them through this transition. And the baby..." She had let the sentence trail off, not wanting to share her opinion about that dear, sweet little Ruthie. There was no sense in deliberately upsetting him. He had enough to deal with already.

But she had noticed that a cloud seemed to pass over his face, the darkness expressing his displeasure. "This is my house, Faith." His tone had been even and low but a stern reminder. "My family."

"Yes," Faith had agreed. "I am aware of that, Manuel. And I respect it, too. But there is no shame in having someone help a bit. Besides," she added as she started the car. "I miss her, too. Maybe this is just as much to heal me as to help you."

That had been the end of their conversation. In fact, there had been no further discussion at all. Instead, Faith had spared him an understanding smile as she shifted the car into drive and slowly headed out of the driveway toward the main road. In her rearview window, she saw him standing there, staring after her with a look of abandonment on his face. She wished she knew exactly what he was thinking, wished that she had been around more during his marriage to Rebecca, but she knew that hindsight was 20-20. All she could do was correct the future, not change the past.

Now, two weeks later, as she stood at the edge of the garden, two weeks into the summer, she stared down at the flourishing vegetables and smiled to herself. She took a moment to say a silent prayer, thanking God for giving her this opportunity to make up to Rebecca for the distance that had grown between them. Even if Manuel didn't appreciate or participate in the healing process, Faith knew that her presence was creating a positive impact on the kinner. And, as far as Faith was concerned, that was the most important thing. Rebecca's kinner needed to get back on track so that they could face the future.

Wiping her hands on her dress, she turned and started to walk toward the house. Thankfully, Anna had volunteered to wash the laundry and had already hung the wet clothes on the line to dry. Faith wasn't looking forward to tackling that chore, not with a diesel powered wringer washer. Besides, Faith had promised the girls that she would take them to the dry goods store after dinner. Anna wanted to buy some material for quilting and Mary was looking for yarn to crochet an afghan. Knowing Sadie, Faith suspected she just wanted to ride along in the car.

As she turned the corner of the house, she noticed that Manuel was hitching up the horse to the buggy. She hadn't seen him yet that day. He tended to make himself scarce whenever she was around. The only time she would see him was during the noon meal, if then. It wasn't that he was unpleasant; just avoiding her and what she symbolized, Faith presumed. It didn't bother her. As she kept reminding herself, she wasn't doing this for Manuel but for Rebecca and those children.

"You going somewhere?" Faith called out, approaching him instead of disappearing into the house.

Manuel looked up, his blue eyes tired and weary. His beard looked grayer than she remembered. And he was thin. He had lost a lot of weight. Faith realized that he was aging right before her eyes. The loneliness was killing him, or, rather, he was allowing it to sap the life out of him. The expression on his face tore through her and she wished she knew him better, wished that she could shake him and tell him that this was not what Rebecca would have wanted for him. But Faith knew that she couldn't do that.

"Mule's mower strap broke," he said, pointing to a leather strap on the ground. "Need to go to the harness shop to get it fixed."

"You'll miss dinner," she pointed out.

He shrugged. "Won't starve, I reckon."

Faith frowned, wishing she felt comfortable enough to tell him that the last thing he needed was to miss a meal. "No, but you'll get sick." Since Rebecca's death, he had already lost too much weight. Faith had noticed that a while back, although she wasn't certain if it was grief, poor eating, or hard work that had shed his pounds. Either way, she was working hard to solve that problem. With a quick glance at her car, Faith extended an olive branch. "Let me take you. It'll be faster."

He hesitated. She could see him trying to figure out how to argue with her, how to avoid spending the time with her.

"Let me go get my purse," she said, taking advantage of the silence to make the decision for him. Within minutes, she was back. She had told Anna that she was taking their daed to the store and could she please watch the other kinner? Faith wasn't certain of how long they would be gone but certainly it couldn't take too much time to repair a harness strap for the mower.

Once in the car, she felt strange to be in such a confined space with Manuel. She realized how little she knew about him. Oh, growing up she had seen him when she was hanging around with Rebecca. They had spoken several times. He had even given her a ride home to her farm on a few occasions. And, of course, there had been the pond incident, one that she tried to forget about, rather than remember. But, after Rebecca had married Manuel, there hadn't been much interaction. Rebecca had morphed into the perfect Amish wife and mother while Faith had transformed into a typical Englische career woman, focused on her education and, later, on teaching her students.

"Turn right up here," he said solemnly, pointing at a road up ahead.

She put on her blinker and slowed the car down before turning. "Sure is good weather for mowing," she said, trying to break the ice.

"Ja," he admitted.

Silence.

"The boys helping you?"

Manuel took a sharp intake of air. "Gideon, ja."

She glanced at him. "You need more help? Perhaps Anna, Mary and I could help. I haven't done haying since I was a teenager with my father. Always loved the smell of fresh cut hay."

"No need," he replied.

Faith sighed. She wasn't making much headway with Manuel and his monosyllabic answers were taxing her nerves.

"I'm sure you could use some help…if not some company," she finally said. She sensed the tension in his lack of a response. "Would be good for Anna, too. She's always in the house. Fresh air, field work…a good medicine for all of us." She was trying to sound light and cheerful, not bossy or strong-headed.

The harness store was only a ten-minute drive from Manuel's farm, down several long, winding back roads. But it would certainly have taken him a good forty five minutes to drive the horse and buggy there. She was glad that she was able to save him that time.

Once she parked the car in the driveway, he got out, not inviting her inside. Nonplussed, she shrugged and opened the car door, jumping out in order to follow behind Manuel. She was just two steps behind him when he opened the door to the harness shop, a small bell tingling to announce their arrival. He hadn't noticed she was behind him and didn't hold the door open for her. Faith reached her hand out to stop it from slamming shut in her face. He paused and looked over his shoulder at her, surprised to see her right behind him. But he said nothing as they continued toward the counter.

"Manuel!" the Amish man said, smiling at him. "Right gut to see you!"

Manuel nodded.

"How you getting on, then?"

Faith cringed at the question but noticed that Manuel did not have any reaction beyond replying with a curt, "Getting on." He lifted the harness strap and set it on the counter, ignoring the way that the man looked at Faith. "Mule just broke this. You have another one?"

The man picked up the strap and looked at it. "Ja, ja," he said, nodding his head. "Sure can't do much mowing with that, now, can you?"

Manuel shook his head. "Nee."

The man tugged at his beard, his eyes glancing at Faith again. She met his eyes and didn't back down. Certainly the man was wondering who she was but, if Manuel wasn't going to introduce them or say anything, neither would she. "Right then," he finally said. "Give me a minute and I'll get it."

Faith watched as the man shuffled away from the counter and through a doorway. She took a moment to begin wandering around the store, looking at the different types of equipment and harnesses on display. Some of the collars were fancy, thick black leather with shiny silver ornamentation on them. Others were just plain, more along the lines of what she was familiar with seeing on the back roads of Pequea.

"That's beautiful," she whispered, more to herself than to Manuel as she reached a hand out to touch the silver studding along the collar.

"Not very practical," she heard him respond. Surprised, she looked up and noticed that he was watching her. "And quite dear."

"I imagine so," she said, knowing that the Amish weren't into the showy trappings that so often caught the attention of the rest of the world. This fancy collar was certainly not for an Amish man. "But it's pretty nonetheless," she said softly as she dropped her hand and walked back to the counter, standing quietly beside him.

She heard him clear his throat, as if he was going to say something. But, it was at that moment that the Amish man came back, carrying a new strap in his hand. "Last one in that size, Manuel." He slid it across the counter. "Don't be breaking anymore straps today," he teased.

The ride back to the farm was quiet, Manuel holding the strap in his hand and staring out the window. She wondered what he was thinking, wondered why he was always so quiet around her. When would the healing process begin?

"I remember a time," she heard herself start to say, "when we were younger and Rebecca and I were helping her daed with the haying. He'd mow and we'd rake the hay into long piles to dry. She loved to hay."

"I know," Manuel said, his voice flat.

Faith glanced at him. "She helped you?"

"Of course," he snapped, shooting a fierce look in her direction. "Everyone helps at hay time on the farm!"

"Then you should certainly be thankful for our help this afternoon," Faith said gaily, ignoring the tone in Manuel's voice as she pulled into the driveway. Putting the car into park, she turned and smiled at Manuel. He didn't look amused at having been trapped. "Guess I'll see about dinner and tell the children about our plans for the afternoon," she said. When he didn't respond, she opened the car door and got out, hurrying to the house to see about finishing the preparation for the noon meal.

Anna clapped her hands in delight when Faith told her. Raking hay meant time outdoors with her daed. She laughed and spun around in the kitchen. "That's wunderbaar gut, Faith! Just like last summer with Mamm. We always had a fun time, singing and laughing! Danke, danke!" the girl gushed. "It won't be the same without Mamm but I'm ever so thankful you talked Daed into it!"

The look of joy on Anna's face made everything worthwhile. Faith smiled, unable to express what she was feeling as Anna glowed, bustling about the kitchen to set the table and help Faith prepare the rest of the meal. When the other children came downstairs, Anna was quick to tell them about Faith's announcement.

Sadie didn't seem as happy as Anna but Mary smiled and glowed in her quiet shy way. "Just like when Mamm was alive," she said softly.

"It's time to hay!" Rebecca told Faith, jumping up and down. "Daed said I can help. You can, too!"

Faith had to laugh at her friend's excitement. While she enjoyed haying with her own father, she never experienced the same jubilance that Rebecca did. Of course, Faith's father used gasoline powered farm equipment while Rebecca's used equipment that was animal powered. She had to admit to harboring a touch of curiosity about helping the Yoder's with the haying, eager to see how different it was when using the mule-drawn equipment.

They spent the morning helping Rebecca's daed, riding along in the mule-drawn mower, their bare feet on the seat as they stood next to her daed. He let them take turns holding the reins and driving the mules under his watchful eye. Faith loved the feel of the leather in her hands, knowing that she was steering those magnificent 18h Belgian mules with the creamy colored fur and large ears. She immediately decided that she preferred the Amish manner of cutting hay to that of her father's method. It was relaxing and fun, a time of bonding with Rebecca and nature.

At the end of the day, Faith thanked Rebecca's daed.

"You come help anytime," he laughed at her, his eyes twinkling. "We'll make you Amish yet, young Faith."

It was almost four when they had finished mowing the backfield. Soon it would be time for the evening milking and Faith needed to prepare supper for the Petersheim's before she would return to her parents' farm. Anna, Mary, and Faith took turns watching Ruthie while the others helped Manuel. As the hay was cut, the children raked it into neat lines for drying. In a few days, they would bale the hay but only after it was properly dried. Hay that had even the slightest bit of moisture was apt to burn when baled and left to smolder in the barn. Many a barn had burned down due to overzealous baling without the proper drying time.

Faith had stood under a tree, holding Ruthie in her arms and watching the rest of the Petersheim family working together. Gideon stood beside Manuel, learning from his daed how to drive the mules. She smiled as she watched, remembering too well when Rebecca's daed had taught her in much the same way. After a while, Manuel had slowed the horses down and looked around, his eyes stopping on his youngest son. With a nod of his head, Manuel had indicated that it was now Benjamin's turn to learn.

Faith had never seen Benjamin smile so broadly.

A family that works together, stays together, she told herself as she carried Ruthie back to the house to get a jump-start on preparing supper. She could hear the family singing a hymn as she crossed the slight hill toward the barn. Ruthie cooed in her ear, pulling at her long braid that hung down her back. Faith wasn't certain which music she appreciated more: the family enjoying themselves or the baby singing in her ear.

It was later that afternoon, as Faith prepared the evening meal, a light fare of bread, applesauce, fruit, and cold cuts, that Manuel approached her. The rest of the children were outside and Ruthie was wiggling on the floor, laying on a blanket in a sunbeam that came through the window. Faith sensed Manuel's presence before she turned and saw him standing there, watching her, from the doorway again. She had been setting the table for the family and now, stood up and faced him.

"I don't know why you are doing this," Manuel said slowly, holding his straw hat in his hand. She bit her lip, waiting for his next words, fully expecting him to banish her from the farm. Instead, however, he nodded his head. "But I am most thankful, Faith." He paused, searching for the right words. She waited patiently, allowing him the time to clear his thoughts. Finally, he looked back at her and sighed. "My family needed you. Danke." And, with that, he turned and disappeared back outside.

Faith stood there for a moment, repeating his words in her mind. He was so sincere, so humbled, in how he had spoken to her. The inner conflict that he had when it came to accepting her help as they healed seemed to be breaking. He was seeing the change in his children and his home. It was no longer a dark and sad place but one that, despite everyone missing Rebecca, could once again be filled with laughter and happiness. And he appreciated that knowledge.

For a moment, Faith fought the urge to cry. She lifted her eyes and stared at the ceiling, blinking for just a moment. *Oh Rebecca,* she thought. *They miss you so. I am just thankful that I can help put your family back on track. Thank you for guiding me here.*

Her heart was light as she finished setting the table for the Petersheim family, pausing to place a small cup filled with freshly cut lilacs in the center. Standing back, she appraised the result: a table for the family filled with love. Satisfied, she smiled to herself and went to gather her things in order to return to her parents' farm, knowing that the family needed this time to enjoy each other's company alone over the suppertime meal.

Chapter Six

When Ruthie smiled at her for the first time, a real sincere smile that was born from recognition, Faith thought that her heart would break into pieces. She scooped the baby into her arms and nuzzled her neck, delighting to hear the gentle cooing noise that Ruthie made. She had been smiling for two weeks now but nothing like the one that the baby blessed Faith with as she walked into the house on this Monday morning.

"Why, good morning to you too, precious!" Faith said. "You look mighty happy today!"

"She slept all night through," Anna said, a look of relief on her face.

"Wow." Faith hugged Ruthie against her chest, kissing the side of the baby's head. "Gave your big sister a break, didn't you?"

The three-month old gurgled and waved her hands in the air, reaching out to pull at Faith's hair. Laughing, Faith reached up to free her braid from Ruthie's tight grasp.

"You should wrap that," Anna said.

"Wrap it?"

"Ja," Anna nodded. "In a bun. She won't be able to pull at it anymore." Anna paused, hesitating before making the offer. "Would you like me to do it?"

The offer was sincere. Faith immediately wondered how often Anna and Rebecca had shared similar moments, a moment of maternal intimacy that touched her heart. Without saying a word, she nodded, recognizing the implications of the offer from the young girl: a bonding moment.

Within minutes, Anna had disappeared into the downstairs bathroom and returned with some pins. Faith smiled to herself as she sat down on the bench by the table, turning her back to Anna so that she had better access to her braid. She shut her eyes as Anna quickly twisted and turned the hair, sticking pins into it so that she had a nice, neat bun at the nape of her neck.

"Why, you almost look Amish," someone said from the doorway.

Faith turned her head, startled to see Gideon and Manuel standing there. Gideon laughed at his own comment, unaware of the expression on his daed's face. Clearly Gideon's remark had struck a chord with Manuel, one that caused that all-too-familiar cloud to cover his eyes. Faith was beginning to recognize it as the expression of deep reflection. Perhaps even conflict. Whenever he had that look, she wondered what he was thinking and wished that she felt comfortable enough around him to inquire further. But she didn't.

"Well," Faith said lightly, trying to make light of Gideon's comment. "I'm sure most Amish don't wear braided buns, now do they?"

"I said *almost*," Gideon teased.

Changing the subject, Faith turned her attention back to Ruthie. "I do believe she smiled at me today, and not a gassy smile but really recognized me!"

Gideon bounced across the room, leaning over Faith's shoulder to look at his baby sister. "She probably thinks you're her mamm," he whispered, but it was loud enough for everyone to hear.

Without looking, Faith knew that Manuel had heard and the comment did not sit well with him. The squeak of the screen door attested to that fact. He had left the house. She wanted to sigh, to shake her head. *Would he ever appreciate what she was trying to do?* But she was doing this for the children, for the memory of Rebecca. Manuel's approval was at the bottom of the list of priorities, she reminded herself.

"I think today is a good day for gardening, don't you agree?" Faith said, directing the question at Anna. "It's cool this morning. And I noticed some of the beans are ready."

After preparing a quick breakfast for everyone, Faith hurried upstairs to change Ruthie. She stared at the smiling baby and, in the privacy of the room, wondered if Gideon was correct. Could the baby think she was the mamm? At what age would the baby truly know? Tickling the baby's bare toes, Faith smiled at her. At what point would Faith begin to think that she was, indeed, the mamm. In many ways, she felt that way with the baby. After all, she had been there at the birth, the only one to pay attention to the newborn while everyone else was so focused on Rebecca.

Ruthie needed to be loved.

Faith was happy to oblige.

"Come on, Faith!" Rebecca called from the other side of the bedroom door. "We want to see!"

"No!"

Rebecca laughed and said something in Pennsylvania Dutch to her brother, James, who was waiting with his sister. When James responded, Faith felt her cheeks flush. They were making fun of her, dressing her up like an Amish girl. She hadn't *wanted to play along but Rebecca had insisted. "You'd make a beautiful Amish girl," she had said. "I want to see how you'd look, anyway!"*

Now, Faith was sorry she had agreed. They were too old for such games. However, it had started after the haying last summer. When Rebecca's daed commented about making Faith Amish, Rebecca had begun to tease her about it. Yet, Faith often wondered how much truth was hidden behind her jovial jests. After all, Rebecca had hinted that, if Faith became Amish, she could marry her older brother James and they'd be true sisters.

They were too young for such talk and silly dreams. But that talk and those dreams lead up to this moment: Faith locked in Rebecca's room wearing a pink Amish dress with a black apron around her waist and a crisp white prayer kapp covering her hair which was pulled back. Faith didn't mind showing Rebecca, but James? The color crept to her cheeks at the thought of it.

"Wie gehts?" another voice said from the other side of the door. Someone else had joined Rebecca and James.

"Manuel!" Rebecca cried out happily. "You have to stay to see this! We've dressed up Faith!"

James laughed. "I want to see the Mennonite-Amish girl!"

Faith leaned against the door and shut her eyes. Manuel? The last person she would want to see in such a state. He would think she was a silly little girl, playing dress up with Rebecca.

She heard Manuel say something in Pennsylvania Dutch to which James laughed again and Rebecca began wiggling the doorknob. "We aren't leaving until you come out, Faith. Please? You promised!"

Reluctantly, Faith counted to ten and took a deep breath. If this was what Rebecca wanted, well she was sure going to give it to her friend. Let them laugh at her. Let them think she was silly! Clenching her teeth, she turned around and reached for the doorknob, hesitating before she unlocked it and flung the door open.

She stood in the doorway, scowling at Rebecca and ignoring the older boys. "There!" she snapped. "Happy now?"

Silence.

Instead, they stood there, staring at her. Even Rebecca seemed taken aback. Faith faced them, her mouth pressed shut as she waited for them to burst out laughing at how she looked. However, it was Manuel who spoke first. A single word escaped his lips when he whispered, "Schee." James raised an eyebrow before lowering his head and backing away from the door. The two older boys quickly disappeared down the staircase into the kitchen but not before Manuel gave her a soft, encouraging smile.

Faith turned to Rebecca. "Is it that hideous?"

Rebecca shook her head. "Nee," she whispered, lowering her eyes.

"What was that word that Manuel said? What did it mean?" Faith demanded, wanting to know what insulting word had been flung at her.

"Schee," Rebecca said, lifting her eyes to look at Faith before she reached for her friend's hand and gave her a smile of approval. "It means beautiful."

The only chore that Faith did not grow to enjoy was the laundry. To Faith, it seemed to be a never ending and thankless task. She found that it was best to do it three times a week rather than twice a week as her mother and most Amish women did. After all, working on a farm was dirty work, from weeding gardens to mucking stalls to chasing cows through the pasture. She began to fall into the routine of washing clothes on Mondays and Fridays while saving sheets and towels for Wednesday.

"I don't understand this machine," she lamented to Anna. "It doesn't make sense!"

Anna tried to keep a straight face while Sadie and Benjamin giggled from the floor where they sat, watching the show. "It's fairly simple, Faith," Anna explained. "You fill up the one tub with hot water and soap and the other one with just hot water. When you are finished washing in the soap, you rinse in the cold water."

Faith sighed and rolled her eyes toward the heavens. "Oh, what would I give for just a touch of electricity!"

This caused the two younger children to giggle again.

She scowled at them teasingly. "Go ahead and laugh, you silly gooses. I don't see you up here scrubbing these clothes!" Then, as if an idea had just struck her, she put her finger to her lips and raised her eyebrows. "Well, if that isn't the greatest idea! Whoever giggles next at me is going to wash all of these clothes by his or herself!"

Both of their faces quickly turned into somber expressions and they sat up straight, quietly watching without so much as a smirk on their faces.

"Ah ha," Faith said, winking at Anna, who smiled. "I thought so."

She was grateful for Anna's help with the laundry but had been determined to figure it out on her own. After all, her purpose in spending her summer days helping the Petersheim family was to help alleviate the responsibility of the many duties that rested on Anna's shoulders.

It was Wednesday and she had decided that she would get the sheets and towels done by herself, without any help from Anna. However, the children lingered around to make certain she was doing it properly. While Faith appreciated their company, their presence made her nervous.

After filling up the two tubs with water, Faith sprinkled some store bought soap into the one tub. When she turned it on, the noise was overpowering as the water churned the soap and made a sudsy mixture.

"I don't think I could ever get used to that," she mumbled, cringing at the loud noise from the diesel fuel engine. "My word!"

Mary placed her arm on Faith's and looked up, their eyes meeting. "You would, Faith. Believe me. It's not that noisy after you get used to it."

There was something of a pleading in Mary's eyes, a look that requested understanding. Recognizing it, Faith smiled and nodded. "You're right, Mary. It just will take some time," she said gently, despite feeling otherwise. "I'm not used to such rumblings and grumblings from a washing machine!" When the two children on the floor giggled, she turned to look at them, pretending to be offended. "What did I just hear? Giggling?"

Immediately, they sobered and Faith had to hide her own smile, amused at their childish antics. "Nothing," Sadie said, reaching for Benjamin's hand. "Nothing at all, Faith."

It took her twice as long to wash the sheets and put them through the wringer. But, when she had a basket full of clean sheets, Faith smiled victoriously at her audience. "See? You can achieve anything once you put your mind to it!" she declared.

Sadie wrinkled her nose, making a face at the comment. "It's just laundry," she said drily.

"That's where you are wrong," Faith said, shaking a finger at the little girl. "It was a challenge, something I didn't want to do, something I didn't know *how* to do. But now, I conquered the challenge, I better understand the machine, and I will be able to do it even faster on Friday!"

Sadie shrugged and leaned over toward Benjamin, whispering, "I still say it's just laundry."

Pretending to scowl at Sadie, Faith swept the basket of damp clothes into her arms and carried it outside, humming as she started to hang the sheets on the clothesline. When she had finished pinning each sheet to the line, she stood back and assessed her work. The sun shone down on the sheets, which waved gently in the summer breeze. With barely any clouds in the sky, she knew that the sheets would be dry in a few hours. She'd be able to fold them and put them away before she left that evening.

"It's going to rain," a voice said behind her.

Faith turned around, surprised to see Manuel watching her. She wondered how long he had been standing there near the corner of the house, his arms crossed over his chest and his straw hat in his hand. "Rain?" She looked up into the sky. It was blue with a few clouds near the top of the hill but nothing that indicated rain. "Do you think so?"

He nodded and pointed toward the sky. "Cumulus clouds. Going to rain later."

Raising an eyebrow, she looked back at the hill. Now that he had pointed it out, she saw the white clouds with the flat bottoms. "Oh help," she muttered. Turning back to Manuel, she asked, "How much time do you think?"

He shrugged. "Hour or two, I reckon."

"Well, at least I have that, I suppose," she sighed.

"I suppose," he said before he slid his straw hat back onto his head and started to walk back toward the barn.

For the next hour, Faith worked in the kitchen and continued to glance out the window. True to Manuel's word, the skies began to grow darker to the point that the house grew shadowy. She wandered to the door, peering out the screen door and felt a cool breeze on her face. The air smelled like rain. She noticed Manuel standing near the opened barn door, unknowingly mimicking her as he stared into the grey sky.

When the first lightning flash lit up the sky, Faith jumped. A few seconds later, a long, low rumble followed.

"Oh help!" she mumbled and pushed open the screen door, hurrying back onto the porch to begin to pull in the line of drying sheets.

The drizzle began to fall from the sky as she unpinned the first sheet. Tossing it into the basket with the pins, she pulled the line and reached for the second sheet. To her surprise, she sensed someone behind her. Glancing over her shoulder, she bumped into Manuel.

"Let me help," he said, reaching for the line and pulling the next sheet off. He moved quickly, wheeling the line and grabbing the pins while she quickly took the sheet. With both of them working at it, it only took a few minutes to rescue the drying sheets before the next lightning flash.

Manuel picked up the basket and carried it inside for Faith.

"You were right," she said.

"Hmm?" He set the basket on the floor in the washroom.

"Oh, the rain. Ja, I reckon I was."

He stood there for a moment, staring at her.

"Thank you for helping me," she said in order to break the silence.

He nodded. "Anna and Mary can help you hang them in the grossdaadihaus," he said.

By the third lightening flash, Sadie and Benjamin raced down the stairs and collided into Faith. Benjamin wrapped his hands around her legs and Sadie clung to her arm. "Now, now," she said, kneeling down to hold them. "What's this about?"

"It's a storm!" Benjamin mumbled, his face pressed against her.

"I know it's a storm," she laughed. "But why the fuss?"

Manuel ran his hand over his face. "Sadie. Benjamin. It's just a storm."

Faith looked up, questioning Manuel with her eyes.

He lowered his hand and exhaled, exasperated. "They are afraid of storms."

Glancing out the open door, Faith studied the sky. In just the past few minutes, it had grown black and the winds had picked up. "Well, it is rather nasty out there," she said. Turning her attention back to the children, Faith gathered them into her arms and hugged them. "Don't worry. You're safe in the house."

"Who's going to milk the cows?" Benjamin asked, his eyes wide and frightened.

The question surprised her. "Why, your daed, of course!"

"Then he'll be outside when he goes to the barn!"

Ah, she thought. Now I understand. Glancing up at Manuel from where she knelt on the floor, she raised an eyebrow, encouraging him to speak. Say anything, she willed silently, just reassure them.

The sky lit up again and a sharp crack quickly followed.

"Mayhaps your daed can stay inside for a spell," Faith finally offered. "I can make him a nice cup of coffee and you two can count how far away the storm is."

Sadie looked at her quizzically. "How do we do that?"

Standing up, Faith took their hand and led them back into the kitchen. Gideon was napping on the sofa while Mary sat on the chair, crocheting a doily. "Well, whenever you see a flash, you slowly count until you hear the thunder. For every five seconds, that's one mile," she explained.

Anna was walking down the stairs, carrying Ruthie. She overheard what Faith said. "I never heard that before!"

"It's true," Faith affirmed, although not fully convinced as to whether or not this was but a popular myth. But at least she had thought of a way to dispel the children's fears, she pondered. Gesturing toward the kitchen window, she added "Come. Let's do it together!" She hoisted the two smaller children so that they could sit on the counter then reached out to take Ruthie from Anna, pausing to nuzzle the baby's neck. Then, while holding Ruthie, Faith leaned forward and peered outside. The children leaned against her, Sadie resting her hand on Faith's shoulder.

Within the next minute, the lightning flash came and, slowly, the four of them counted to six before the thunder could be heard.

"That's just over a mile away, then!" Anna exclaimed, excited with this new game.

"That's right," Faith said, smiling at her. "Let's see who can calculate the next strike!"

For the next ten minutes, the children stared out the window while Faith put on some water to make Manuel coffee. She rubbed Ruthie's back while she waited for the kettle to boil and watched Sadie, Benjamin, and Anna peering outside. She glanced over at Gideon, still stretched out on the sofa and oblivious to the excitement in the house. Sweet Mary kept her head bent, working diligently on her crocheting despite the room being so dark. Faith's heart swelled with love for the children.

And then she caught sight of Manuel. He hadn't sat at the table. Instead, he leaned against the doorframe, having watched her with the children as she took charge of their fears, creating a game to divert their attention from what frightened them so. When her eyes met his, he held her gaze for a long moment and Faith caught her breath. In the dark shadows of the room, he seemed to fill the doorway with a larger presence than she remembered seeing before. She couldn't tell whether he was pleased or not with what she had done, although he seemed to be considering her as he watched her.

"Coffee, Manuel?" she managed to say.

"Danke." His reply was soft and he continued to stare at her.

Faith handed Ruthie to Anna so that she could prepare a mug of coffee for Manuel. Under his steady eye, she felt nervous moving about the kitchen. She wasn't used to him being in the house. Normally, he stayed outside, working in the barn or the fields. Having him in the kitchen while she worked was unnerving.

"Ooo, there's another one and that sure was bright!" Benjamin cried out.

"One...two...three..." Sadie counted out loud before the

noise stopped her. She glanced at Faith. "That's closer then, ain't so?"

Carrying the mug of coffee, Faith walked over to Manuel. He hadn't moved from where he stood and continued to follow Faith with his eyes. When she handed him the mug, he seemed to hesitate before reaching out to take it from her. Raising one eyebrow, he gave a simple nod of his head. "Danke, Faith," he said, his voice low.

The next lightning strike was immediately followed by a loud crack and Sadie shrieked, covering her ears. Within seconds, more thunder rumbled, low and deep. The windows rattled and Faith felt as if she could feel the reverberation of the thunder within her body. "That sure was close," she said and walked back to the window, looking outside. "Best step back from the window. Just in case."

Sadie and Benjamin scampered off the counter.

"I saw that lightning bolt," Benjamin said, the color draining from his face. He turned to look at his father, his eyes wide with fright. "It looked like it went over to the neighbor's farm!"

Manuel nodded at his son. "Once the storm passes, we can ride over to make certain everyone's alright, then." He sipped at his coffee, his eyes meeting Faith's once again. "Anna, you should help Faith hang those sheets over in the grossdaadihaus. They won't dry proper in the basket."

Ten minutes later, when Faith returned with Anna from the small grossdaadihaus, the sky was beginning to lighten again and Manuel was gone from the kitchen. Faith felt a sense of relief that he had left the house and, twenty minutes later, when she heard the horse and buggy rattle down the driveway, she knew that he had gone to check on his neighbors. She breathed a sigh of relief, knowing that he wouldn't be back for a while. Apparently, Sadie and Benjamin had ridden along with him, too.

She needed a few minutes to collect her thoughts. Comforting the children had stirred something within her. The fact that they had come to her when they were scared and relied on her to reassure them that nothing would happen had touched her. She also knew that their reaction had not gone unnoticed by Manuel and, based on her own reaction, she knew that it bothered him.

Over the past few weeks, she had grown attached to the children. Each one had their individual personality. When summer ended, Faith knew that she'd hate to say goodbye. She was enjoying herself much more than she had thought possible, finding happiness in the small things such as leaving fresh cut flowers on the table before she left in the evening or seeing Anna's smile in the morning when she arrived. The conversations that the children engaged in during the day often brought a smile to her face. And Ruthie...

Faith's heart broke when she thought of leaving Ruthie at the end of the summer. In just a few months, the baby would begin sitting up and then crawling. One day she would stand and take her first, wobbly steps. Faith knew that she couldn't be there to see those milestones and the realization that she would miss them brought tears to her eyes.

"Faith?" Anna asked. "You alright?"

With a forced smile, Faith nodded her head. "Of course," she answered. "Just thinking about what to make for supper tonight."

It was almost an hour later when Manuel returned. Sadie and Benjamin ran into the house first. They were full of energy and overly excited about something. It took a few minutes to get them to calm down before they could explain what they had seen.

Sadie finally blurted out, "The neighbors! Their tree in the yard, that big old oak tree, was hit by lightning and pieces of the tree fell onto the house!"

Faith gasped. "No one was hurt, I hope!"

Sadie shook her head. "Nee, no one was hurt."

"Thank the Lord!"

Manuel walked into the room and headed over to where Gideon still slept. He tousled his son's hair, calling his name in order to rouse him. "Gid," he said. "Need your help at the Zook's farm." He looked at Anna. "You should come, too."

"Why, I think they could use all of our help," Faith said. "Are they planning to try to fix it today?"

Manuel frowned at her offer. "Have to get the limb down first. See how much damage there is. No need for the younger ones to go."

Faith saw the disappointed look in Sadie's face. She reached out and touched the little girl's shoulder and, when Sadie looked up, Faith smiled. "We'll do something nice for the family, then. We can make a nice casserole to take over to them. Surely they will be preoccupied and won't have time to think about supper." That idea seemed to appease Sadie for she grinned and nodded. "You can help me take it over there later, ok?"

It was almost three o'clock when Sadie and Faith walked down the road toward the Zook's farm. Mary had volunteered to stay home with Ruthie and Benjamin. Skipping down the road, her bare feet dirty on the heels, Sadie held Faith's hand and pointed out the different birds that she saw along the way. The sun lingered in the sky, its rays warm on Faith's face. She inhaled deeply, smelling the fresh air.

"I love summer time," Sadie said. "Don't you, Faith?"

"Oh yes," Faith responded, squeezing Sadie's hand a little to emphasize her words. "I love the sunshine and the flowers and the time to relax."

"You like working?"

Good question, Faith thought as she looked down at Sadie's sweet face. "Well, I like teaching, that's for certain," Faith finally responded.

Pursing her lips as if thinking hard about something, Sadie was quiet for a moment. Faith turned her attention back to the road, directing the little girl closer to the grass when a car drove up behind them. It was disappearing around the bend when Sadie finally asked what was on her mind. "You ever going to get married, Faith?"

Another good question, she thought. She hadn't dated much in her life, no one seriously. She found that most of the men in her circles were not very interesting. "I suppose one day," Faith said with a sigh. "It's not high on my priority list, though."

"Why not?"

Indeed, Faith said to herself. *Why not?* "Well," she started cautiously. "I like living on the farm and helping my father with the cows and haying. And I love being with the children that I teach. I don't think I'd like to give up being with children."

"Mayhaps you could do both!"

Faith smiled and quickly changed the subject. "Is that a bluebird I see on the box by the telephone pole?"

Ten minutes later, they were walking up to the Zook's

house. The men were already on the roof, hammering shingles over a freshly constructed patch over the kitchen. Outside on a picnic table, Anna was pouring lemonade into a cup and handing it to the Zook's older son. Faith smiled to herself, recognizing the look in Anna's eye as Jonas thanked her for the refreshment, quickly drinking it and wiping his mouth on the back of his hand.

"Faith!" Anna called out when she noticed Faith and Sadie approaching. "You should have seen that hole in the roof! They are quite lucky no one was hurt."

Setting the basket down on the picnic table, Faith turned around and looked up, her eyes quickly taking in the scene of Manuel, Gideon, and the senior Zook finishing up the work on the roof. She noticed Manuel pause and rub his forehead before glancing down to where Faith stood with his daughters. He seemed to contemplate her standing there, a strange look on his face, a look that she had seen only one time before: the *Schee* day, the day Rebecca had dressed Faith in Amish clothing.

Miriam Zook walked out the open kitchen door and frowned when she saw Faith standing there. It took her a moment to recognize the Englischer standing among the children. "You're Rebecca's friend, then?" she asked as she approached Faith. She was a large Amish woman with greying hair protruding from beneath her prayer kapp. Faith recognized her from the funeral and knew that she was a busy woman with ten children, the two older daughters already married and with babies. "The one who has been helping out with the kinner this summer, ja?"

Faith smiled, introducing herself. "We met at the funeral, I think," she added.

Crossing her arms over her big bosom, Miriam shook her head and glanced at Sadie who was already busy picking up small pieces of shingles that had been tossed to the ground. "Such a tragedy, that," Miriam said with a loud sigh. "Those poor kinner. And to think that Anna is approaching her time without a mamm." She shook her head and clicked her tongue, a look of sorrow on her face.

Faith glanced over at Anna who was helping Sadie. The young girl continued to steal glances at Jonas, unbeknownst to the object of her affection. "Yes, that is sad," Faith admitted, her heart heavy as she said the words. Then, trying to lighten the subject, Faith gestured toward the basket. "Sadie and I made you a casserole for supper. Figured you might be too busy to cook with all of this activity."

"That was right nice of you," Miriam said, looking into the basket. "Good of Manuel to come check on us after that storm."

Faith nodded. "That was some storm, wasn't it? Blew in so fast!"

"Ja, that it did!" she affirmed, nodding her head. "Wonder how Manuel knew?"

"Oh that was the children's doing! We were watching the storm by the kitchen window. It was Benjamin who saw the lightning strike and told his daed," Faith explained.

"Did he, now?" Miriam seemed surprised to hear that. "He's always been so scared of storms!"

Faith laughed. "I taught him a trick to calculate the distance of the lightning and that seemed to preoccupy him. Took his mind off of the storm and his fears."

Miriam raised an eyebrow. "Aren't you clever?" Despite the compliment, there was something in Miriam's tone that spoke of an underlying thought as she assessed the Englischer standing before her. "Those kinner must be right attached to you, then," she said casually.

"They're great children," Faith replied, suddenly feeling uncomfortable and wishing Anna would come back to help change the direction of the conversation. Glancing up at the roof, Faith saw that Manuel was still watching her and, without knowing why, she felt the color flood to her cheeks. "Looks like they are almost finished, yes?" She turned away from the house and busied herself with removing the casserole from the basket and handing it to Miriam.

Chapter Seven

Before Faith realized it, August was coming to an end. It had been over four months since Rebecca had passed away and the school year would soon be starting. The kinner would return to their one room schoolhouse and Faith would get back to her own classroom. It broke Faith's heart that Anna would be left at home to care for Ruthie and the house. But try as she might, Faith couldn't come up with a solution.

For two months, she had spent five days a week at the Petersheim's home, cooking and cleaning, washing and gardening. It was a routine that she had become accustomed to and would surely miss, almost as much as she would miss the kinner. Slowly, she had come to learn and appreciate exactly why Rebecca had thrived so much on being a good Amish woman. There was a joy to each day that Faith had never experienced before those weeks spent at the Petersheim's.

So when she walked into the house on that Monday of her last week helping the family, she was surprised to find the house in complete disarray. Gone was the order from Friday when she had left. Dirty dishes were piled high in the sink. Toys were scattered on the floor. And she could hear the baby crying from upstairs.

"What in the world...?" she said aloud even though no one was nearby to hear her words.

She hurried up the stairs to where the baby was, surprised to see her still in the crib in Anna's room. This hadn't been the routine at all, she thought angrily as she picked up Ruthie and tried to console her. With a wet diaper and an empty belly, there was no amount of comfort that Faith could give her. Instead, she quickly changed Ruthie into dry and clean clothing before taking her downstairs to fix her a morning bottle. They sat on the sofa, Ruthie snuggled into Faith's arms, for at least twenty minutes before the other kinner came into the kitchen.

"Where have you been?" Faith demanded. "What has happened here since Friday?"

Anna looked tired and plopped herself into a chair. Resting her cheek on her arm, she stared at Faith. "Daed's sick."

The other children looked just as weary. Sadie and Benjamin crawled onto the sofa next to her, Benjamin leaning against her and shutting his eyes. Faith frowned and realized that, if Manuel was sick, the kinner must have been tending to the dairy by themselves all weekend. That was a lot of cows to milk and manure to shovel for five young children.

"Didn't anyone stop in this weekend to visit or help?" Faith asked.

"Oh ja, Lydia and her family did but Daed told them he didn't need their help, that he was feeling better," Gideon offered.

That didn't surprise Faith. She had seen Manuel's stubborn side. "Where is he now?"

Gideon glanced upstairs, answering her question without words.

After handing Sadie the baby, Faith hurried back upstairs and hesitated outside the door to the main bedroom where Manuel slept. Knocking softly on the door, she quietly opened it and peered inside the dark room. The shades were drawn down and the windows were shut. She was immediately overwhelmed by the scent of illness. Frowning, she went over to the closest window and opened it, lifting the shade enough so she could see her way around the room.

He was sleeping in the bed, the covers up to his chest. He hadn't even heard her enter the room.

Approaching the bed, she said his name softly, hoping to elicit a response.

Nothing.

She reached out her hand and touched his forehead. The temperature of his skin shocked her. He was burning up with fever. "Manuel?" she repeated softly and nudged him with her fingers.

"Rebecca?"

For some reason, the word cut through her. After all that I have done, she thought but stopped herself before she went further. "It's Faith, Manuel. You're burning up. I am going to call the doctor."

"Nee, nee," he started to argue, waving a weak hand at her.

"How long have you been like this?" She didn't wait for an answer as she walked to the doorway and called down the stairwell for Mary to bring her a glass of cool water and a wet cloth. "You need to go see someone for treatment, Manuel."

"I'm fine," he said, his voice weak and barely audible contradicting that very statement through his thick, chapped lips.

Faith waited for Mary and quickly took the glass of water from her. She hurried to the bed and, despite feeling uncomfortable, she sat on the edge of the bed and helped him raise his head so that he could drink the water. "Just a little," she coaxed. "Not too much." Setting down the glass onto the nightstand, Faith waved to Mary to give her the wet cloth. She took it and placed it on Manuel's forehead, her hand pressing it gently against his hot skin. "How long have you been ill?"

"Started Saturday morning," he managed to say. "Got bad yesterday."

She was frustrated. All of her life, she had lived among these people. Yet she still couldn't understand their reluctance to ask for help when needed. "This is ridiculous," she said, mostly to herself. "You need to see a doctor. You need someone to come help you, Manuel. Isn't there someone? A niece?"

He shook his head. "Need to do it myself," he mumbled and let his head fall to the side, the effort of speaking having exhausted him.

Faith lifted the cloth from his head and sighed. "Manuel, when will you learn? People are here to help you." She paused. Why was he so adamant to accepting the assistance of others? Her entire life living next to the Amish had taught her that Amish helped others. Truly, he couldn't be of the mindset that help only went one way and that was from him to others, never to be returned in his direction. *Or perhaps*, she thought, *it's just my help that he doesn't accept.* "I am here to help you," she added hesitantly.

In a surprise gesture, he reached for her hand. The movement was slow but deliberate. His touch on her hand startled her and, for a moment, she almost withdrew it. But then, she remembered that this was Manuel, not some stranger, and he was in need. His eyes, so dull with illness, touched her. "You are a great help, Faith," he whispered and then, shutting his eyes, he sighed as he repeated the words, "Great help."

Looking over her shoulder at Mary, Faith gestured toward the door as she lowered her voice. "More cool water in a basin, sweet Mary. I want to keep his forehead cool until the fever breaks. And ask Anna to cook up some chicken. The broth will do him good."

Without an argument, Mary did as she was instructed, never questioning Faith who remained seated next to her daed on the bed, his hand still covering hers, as he slept.

She stared at him, her eyes beginning to tear up as she thought of the pain that Manuel had been feeling for the past few months. Yet, she had witnessed a humble recovery in him. His words were few and far between but he smiled more often at the children and seemed to draw the boys into his world more frequently. And every so often, Faith would catch him standing in the doorway, silent and relaxed, watching as Faith worked with the girls in the kitchen. A sense of normalcy was returning to the Petersheim farm.

Until now.

With Manuel being sick, how could she return to work, she asked herself? How could she desert the family that she had struggled so hard to help over the past summer? The inner turmoil that she felt, sitting by Manuel's side and having her hand held by him, was deep. Too deep. She shut her eyes and said a prayer, praying for his swift recovery from illness and her swift recovery from the questions that had begun to form in her mind.

For the rest of the morning, she directed the children on what to do, giving them small tasks to begin cleaning the kitchen and preparing a good broth for their daed. She spent the day monitoring him, taking turns with Mary at keeping his forehead cool so that she could escape back to the kitchen, tasting the stock and helping with the mess.

"School starts tomorrow," Anna said glumly as she

helped Faith dry the dishes.

"I know that."

"I won't be returning," Anna added.

Silence. There was nothing to say. Faith leaned her wet hands on the sides of the kitchen sink and gazed out the window. It was a beautiful day. If she hadn't looked at the calendar, she never would have known it was the end of summer. There was a breeze that kept the house cool, despite the sun high overhead. It felt more like spring to Faith. And spring was a time of new beginnings. The very new beginnings that Anna was owed.

"Yes you will," Faith announced, her words short and even.

Anna stopped drying the pan in her hand and stared at Faith.

"I'm taking a leave of absence, Anna." Faith could barely believe that she was saying these words. *A leave of absence.* "Your mother would want you to continue to go to school. It's not fair for you to put your life on hold. And I made a promise, a promise I want nothing more than to keep." Faith turned around and faced Anna. With a smile, a smile filled with love for the eager and hopeful face that stared back at her, Faith reached out and touched Anna's cheek. "So yes, dear Anna, you *will* go back to school."

Three days had passed since Faith had made up her mind and notified the school that she needed to invoke Family Medical Leave. That gave her twelve weeks to continue caring for the Petersheim's until she could figure out her next step. She had quickly gotten into a routine, arriving at the

Petersheim's in time to oversee the preparation of breakfast. After everyone had eaten, she saw the children off to school, her heart warming at the broad, genuine smile Anna bestowed upon her each morning. The gratitude that Anna showed for the sacrifice that had been made in order to insure she could continue her education truly touched Faith.

During the day, Faith spent most of her time split between tending to Ruthie and the regular chores: cleaning, laundry, and cooking. When the children returned home from school, they immediately clamored into the kitchen, eager to tell her about their day while happily snacking on freshly baked bread or sugar cookies. Then, they would hurry to the barn to help with the evening milking, all but Anna who stayed behind to help Faith in the kitchen.

Faith had sensed Anna's need for individual attention over the summer. She seemed to long for time alone with Faith, time to talk or simply to work alongside her. As frequently as possible, Faith tried to send the other children outside or assign them a chore that kept them busy in order to provide Anna with that time. It was more than obvious how much Anna missed her mamm, but it was also obvious that Faith was filling that void.

Manuel noticed it, too. On more than one occasion, he came downstairs in the afternoon, a blanket wrapped around his shoulders, and paused on the bottom step, watching the interaction between Faith and Anna. The first time that Faith caught him watching them, she was startled and hurried over to him.

"You should be in bed, Manuel. If you need something, all you have to do is ask," she fussed.

"Nee, nee," he said. "I'm tired of being up there all day."

But the next day, she once again caught him on the step, watching her and Anna. There was a look on his face, a mixed expression of sadness and wonder at the same time. When she noticed him, she stopped what she was doing and met his eyes. He was looking directly at her but, at the same time, he was looking through her, as if far away and in another world. She couldn't help wonder what made him so preoccupied and pensive. Yet, when she asked if she could get him something, he merely shook his head and retreated to his chair.

It was Thursday when she was sitting on the sofa, giving Ruthie her mid-morning bottle as she felt his eyes lingering upon her. She turned to look and he was leaning against the wall, a blanket over his shoulders and his hair tousled. "Manuel!" she gasped. "You startled me."

He held her gaze for a moment, that distant look once again in his eyes. She wondered where he was.

"Are you alright, then? Can I get you something to eat?"

He shrugged his shoulders. "Nee," he mumbled. "Not hungry just yet."

"Feeling better?"

He nodded. "Ja, I think I'll be strong enough to help the kinner with the evening milking."

At this, Faith frowned. "Don't push yourself, Manuel. You've been through so much. The stress has surely caused you to feel so poorly. If you push yourself, you'll be right back in the same situation."

"Don't want that," he replied and, for the briefest of moments, she wondered what he meant. He was still staring at her, watching her hold the baby while Ruthie sucked at her bottle. "You love that baby, don't you?"

"You mean Ruthie?" She hated how he kept referring to

his little girl as *that baby*. "Your daughter? Why, yes I do!"

"Ruthie," he whispered.

"She's a precious angel," Faith said, peering down at the sweet face of the infant in her arms. "I love her sweet smiles."

"You're good with her," he offered softly. "I can't thank you enough." He paused, looking toward the window for a moment. "It should have been my mamm or Rebecca's that helped out but..." He let the sentence fade without completing it. His mamm had died years ago and Rebecca's mamm was ill. With the sisters busy with their own farms and kinner, Manuel had been left on his own. "You stepped in and saved my family," he added by way of closure.

Faith wasn't certain how to respond to that praise. She lowered her head and felt the color flood to her cheeks. She didn't think of her actions as *saving* the family. She thought of it as the Christian thing to do. No, she corrected herself. She had fallen in love with the family, the children. She did this for Rebecca and for herself. "I think that's mighty high praise, Manuel."

"It's deserved." And with that, he turned and headed back up the stairs to return to his room.

On Friday, Faith felt a new energy about her. The week had passed surprisingly quickly and her routine had created a new peace in her life. Once the children had left for school, Faith gathered their dirty clothing and spent the morning washing and hanging out the clothes. It was a beautiful September day, just warm enough with a breeze so that it was pleasantly comfortable. She stood back and watched the clothes on the line, the girls' dresses so colorful next to the boys' simple black and brown pants.

The rest of the morning, she focused on inside chores,

hoping to free up the afternoon to work outside with the children. It was too nice to be indoors all day. Her mind raced in the quiet, Ruthie having fallen asleep for her mid-day nap a bit early. Even Manuel had ventured downstairs and, after tending to some light chores in the yard that morning, he had returned to take a short nap in his favorite reading chair, by the window. At first, his presence in the kitchen room had made Faith feel on edge. But, when she saw that he was sleeping, she smiled to herself. He was getting better but still needed his rest. It had been a long few months and rest was the best medicine. He needed his sleep in order to get better. He needed to get better so that she could return to her own life.

It was the knock at the door that broke the silence in the kitchen. Glancing at Manuel, she hurried to the door, hoping that whoever was visiting wouldn't wake him. She opened the door and greeted the Amish man standing there with a pleasant "Hello." There was a confused look on the man's face and he seemed startled to find a woman answering the door, especially an Englische woman.

"Where's Manuel?" the man demanded, his brow furrowed in displeasure.

So that's how it will be, she thought. "He's inside but he's been rather sick."

"So I heard."

Faith noticed an edge to the man's voice, a touch of disapproval in his tone. She wondered why. "And you are?"

The man lifted his chin and stared down his nose at her. "The bishop."

Ah, Faith thought, recognizing him now. "Well, do come in," she said pleasantly and stepped back. "I'm sure he'll want to speak with you."

"Did I tell you about that Byler family?"

Faith had never seen Rebecca so agitated. Her face was pale and her hands were shaking. "Do I know them?"

Rebecca shook her head. "Nee," she responded. "I don't think so. They live in another church district. Ja, vell, I heard my parents talking and the bishop won't let their dochder take the kneeling vow!"

Despite not being Amish, Faith understood the serious nature of such a decision. Baptism was an important transition in both the Amish and the Mennonite religions. To be denied that formal entry into the church could mean only one thing: something bad had happened. "Did you find out why?"

Rebecca shook her head. "I don't know everything but she was really not being kind to another girl in their g'may. Made up lies, said bad things, gossiped, bullied Priscilla Smucker!"

"Those are bad things," Faith admitted.

"Susie Byler was supposed to take her instructionals and the bishop forbade it, then removed her from the district!"

For lying? That didn't sound right to Faith. There must have been more to the story than just that. "That seems very severe, don't you think so, Rebecca?"

This time, her friend shrugged. "Those bishops carry a lot of weight within their communities. If he refused her baptism, he certainly had good reasons, I reckon." She chewed on her lower lip, lifting her eyes up to stare at Faith. "I hope I never give the bishop any reason to deny me my kneeling vow or to get shunned. That would just be downright awful!"

She listened to the conversation from the top of the stairs, not understanding one word of what was being said with the exception of her name, Rebecca's name, and the names of the children. However, from the harsh tone and the exchange of words, Faith knew that the bishop was talking to Manuel about Faith's presence in the house. And, from the sound of his voice, it was not a happy conversation.

Leaning against the wall, she shut her eyes and sighed. If only Manuel would get better. If only Manuel would take charge of the children. If only...

Still, she knew that she would miss the children. She had grown to love them, to enjoy their stories and their appreciation for everything that she did. She loved to watch Anna blossom into a young woman. She loved to see shy Mary try to hold her own against the spirited Sadie. Of course, there was also Ruthie, the small bundle of joy that, on some level, Faith had begun to feel as if they belonged together. Hadn't Faith been the first to hold the infant after her birth? Hadn't Faith been the one to turn around the feelings of the children toward their youngest sibling?

And the boys? They were small replicas of Manuel, with those hauntingly blue eyes and brilliant smiles. They had that quick wit about them that reminded Faith of Manuel before Rebecca's death. They were funny and charming and full of life. If only...

"Faith?"

His voice was strained as he called out for her and, the moment that he said her name, he began to cough. She hurried down the stairs and went to the kitchen sink to fetch him a glass of cool water. She was surprised to see that the bishop had left already. How long had she been upstairs? How long had she been daydreaming?

"Better?" she asked, placing a hand on his shoulder as she leaned down to stare into his face. "You still look so flushed, Manuel."

He stared back at her, his eyes dull from his sickness. "You have been taking right gut care of this family, Faith," he started in a soft voice, his gaze steady and stronger than he really felt. "While I mayhaps wasn't too receptive when you arrived, you set this family back on course, for sure and certain. For that, I can't thank you enough."

She didn't respond but reached for the glass of water that he held in his hand. She set it down on the table next to where he sat and waited. Faith could tell that he was getting ready to tell her something and whatever that something was, she wasn't going to like it.

"I reckon it's time that you start taking care of yourself though," he said, his eyes flickering away from hers.

"Is that what the bishop said?" She didn't have to ask the question. She already knew the answer. "Did you ask him who is to tend the farm while you are watching Ruthie? Did you ask him who is to put food on the table at night for the children while they are at school? Who is supposed to do the laundry? And please don't say Anna. The child needs to be in school!"

"Nee," Manuel said softly. "Not Anna." He hesitated before he spoke again. "He did tell me that it's time for me to find another wife, though. A wife to do all of those things, not an Englische woman." He looked at her. "Not an Englische woman who should be doing her own work and living her own life."

A wife? Faith almost choked on the words. "But Rebecca...?"

Manuel shut his eyes and shook his head. She could see that the conversation pained him on many different levels. "That's our way, Faith. You have to understand."

"Is she that easily replaced?"

His eyes opened and he stared at her again. "Nee!" he said, almost shouting the word. "But the children...it's about the children..."

"I'm here!" She said louder than she intended before quickly lowering her voice. "Manuel, I'm here for the children!"

Manuel sighed. "You aren't Amish and you aren't their mamm." He put his hand up to his forehead as if the pain was too much to bear. "They need a new mamm, Faith. The bishop was right and, deep down, we both know it to be true."

Furious, Faith stormed out of the room and outside the door to escape the oppressive nature of the house. How could Manuel let another man dictate how to live his own life? How could Manuel simply replace Rebecca? How could another woman replace their mamm? Her heart beat rapidly and she had to pause, standing on the grass to catch her breath.

You take care of my children. You help Manny.

The last words that Rebecca had spoken. The last request that her friend had made.

You'll come by and visit? Mayhaps even help a bit, ja?

That request from Anna, so hopeful and so full of desperation.

And then it hit her.

For a moment, she stood there, staring into the sky and taking deep breaths. It was a crazy idea, an idea that would change everything. Yet, she knew at once that it was the right thing to do. It was what God wanted her to do. Why He had led her back to Rebecca's life, her family's life.

Please God, she prayed. *Send me a sign if this is Your will.*

"Faith?"

She turned around, staring at Manuel who was leaning against the open door. For a moment, she was struck by him. His blue eyes were watching her, curious and concerned with her reaction to his words. There was a look about him, one that she hadn't noticed before that moment. She was struck by the aura of kindness surrounding him, an aura of acceptance and faith. He had always been that way. Only she was recognizing it now for the very first time.

"Please come back," he said, his voice soft and gentle. "I didn't mean to upset you." He sighed and shook his head. "But the bishop is right. I need to find a new mamm for these kinner. You know it, too. Rebecca would want it. God wants it." He paused before he admitted, "I reckon I want it, too."

The sign.

Faith lifted her chin and crossed the small patch of grass, standing between them. She studied his face for a long while, wondering if she could really do this. Wondering if this was the right thing to say. And, as she pondered this, her heart beating, she heard herself speak the words that had been floating through her mind. "I'll be their new mamm," she declared, "if you ask me to, Manuel". Immediately, she lowered her eyes. She didn't want to see his reaction. She was afraid to look at him for fear that he would think she had lost her mind. In truth, she wasn't certain where the strength had come from for her to say those words. "Rebecca would want it," she whispered. "I think God wants it, too."

Silence.

She glanced back at him, curious to see his response yet dreading it at the same time. As soon as she had said it, she knew that it sounded outrageous. Certainly, he would think she had lost her mind. After all, despite having grown up Mennonite and the daughter of a farmer, she was an educated woman and had a career. To become their new mother meant she would have to give up everything. Yet, she loved the children enough to do just that. She wanted to do this, and not just for the children and Manuel but for Rebecca.

"Manuel?" she asked, waiting for his reaction.

And then he nodded.

For a moment, she felt her heart skip a beat in her chest. Just like that, she realized, with one simple nod of his head. He had agreed and, just like that, they were engaged. Promised to be married. *My future,* she thought. *How different it will be from what I had imagined it!*

She heard Manuel clear his throat. "I'll talk to the bishop," he said slowly, his words careful and slow. "If he agrees, you'll have to meet with him, then. Arrange for an instructional."

"I know that," she said, despite the opposite being true. The one thing that she knew was that she would have to take the Amish baptism and live by their rules. As a wife, she would have to answer to Manuel, release some of her control in obedience to his direction. "I suspected as much, anyway," she admitted, correcting what she had previously said. The entire conversation sounding as if someone else was having it.

"If they agree to give you the baptism," he said, lifting his chin and watching her carefully. "We would be married in November."

Married. The word sounded foreign and strange when

he said it. A surreal feeling overcame her. For a moment, she felt as if she were floating above herself, watching the scene as it unfolded, eavesdropping on the conversation of two strangers. Was she actually agreeing to marry this man, the widower of her best friend? *You help Manny,* Rebecca had said, pleading with her eyes for Faith to agree. Why had she agreed? She didn't even know this man. Yet, she was committing to spend the rest of her life with him. She had just promised to give up all of the conveniences of her Englishe world in order to raise Rebecca's children. All of this, she realized, to make good on the dying wish of her best friend.

"November," Faith whispered.

He took a deep breath and forced a weak smile. "Now, come back inside, then," he said gently. "I reckon this is something we should pray on, ja?"

Faith nodded, feeling weak in the knees. She managed to walk up the stairs to the porch and, with a brief hesitation, slipped past him to return to the kitchen. Behind her, she heard Manuel close the door and walk across the floor. He stood behind her and, when she glanced over her shoulder, feeling completely at a loss of what to say or do, he reached for her hand. When his fingers touched hers, she felt as though an electric shock ran up her arm, a wave of energy and fire, and she shivered. He gestured toward the sofa and led her to it, pausing before he dropped to his knees and placed his hands before a bowed head. Faith took a deep breath and followed his example, kneeling beside him as she silently prayed to God that she was doing the right thing.

O Father, she prayed. *I love You and come to You with thankfulness but at the same time I am overwhelmed. I know that Your desire is to keep this family in the center of Your divine will and to show Your love in a mighty way. O Lord, I love these children like they were my own. Please give me Your blessing and guide me with Your righteous right hand. All good things come from You. My friendship with Rebecca was the start and I miss her so, but her grace has shown me more than I ever imagined about Your love for Your children. Guide me as the mother of these children, let me find love to pour onto this man, the man I have chosen to be my husband and bless me with Your divine beauty. I love You Father. Thank you. Amen.*

It bothered her that she didn't feel stronger when she stood up. She felt drained, both physically and emotionally. Standing beside Manuel, she felt as if she had no idea who he was. Yet, just moments before she had not only agreed to marry him...she was the one who had suggested it! The brazen words that had poured from her mouth shocked her, even now that it was done and agreed upon. Betrothed. Engaged.

What have I done?, she asked herself. Her knees felt weak and she had to put her hand out to steady herself. Manuel saw and reached for her, helping her sit on the sofa.

"Mayhaps I should get you some water, Faith?" he asked, concern showing in his eyes.

She shook her head. She knew that the color had drained from her face as the enormity of the agreement hit her. What would her parents say? What would Rebecca's family think? And it wasn't just agreeing to marry Manuel; it was the complete change in her lifestyle. Yes, she was fairly familiar with the Amish culture and their religion. After all, Mennonites and Amish were religious cousins. But to think that so much would have to change!

Everything would change. Despite the similarities in their religions, the cultural differences were astounding. At the heart of the family was the man and only after him came the woman. Faith had no idea what the next steps might be. Indeed, for the first time, in a long time, she realized that she had just taken the first step of a journey in which she had no control; nor did she have any idea as to how to proceed.

Lifting her eyes, she stared at Manuel. He, too, looked pensive as he watched her. His face was pale and his eyes concerned with her reaction. Suddenly, Faith felt shy in his presence, realizing that, by agreeing to marry Manuel, she had just turned over the authority of her life into his hands. She was no longer the master of her own destiny. Manuel was in charge. "What happens now?"

"Vell," he started, pulling up a chair to sit opposite her. With his legs out, he leaned forward and rested his hands on his knees as he spoke to her. "I reckon I must go speak to the bishop. He will have to agree, like I said, to your baptism. Given the situation and your background, a proving time can be expedited, I reckon."

"Proving time?"

Manuel frowned, more from his own inability to properly explain things to her than anything else. "Proving time. The time when you will need to learn Amish ways, Faith. That will be before your baptism." He glanced at her and tried to smile but he, too, was nervous and could barely even do that. She could see that he was trying to take on his role, the take-charge role of man of the house. But it had been a long time since he had felt that confidence. "This is all new to me, too, ja? Perhaps to everyone in the church district. We have to rely on the bishop to guide us."

"The bishop?" she asked, remembering the stern face of the man who had visited not more than an hour before. Faith found it hard to imagine such a harsh man being about to help her at all.

Manuel nodded. "He will know how to proceed. But first he must agree. Mayhaps he will say no. It's always a possibility and what he decides is final."

Final, she thought. She had never considered that. After all that they had just discussed and decided, someone else might refuse them? She'd never be able to sleep at night, not knowing whether or not she would be the stepmother to those children, children she already considered her own.

"Oh," she whispered.

Reluctantly, he reached out and touched her hand, holding it awkwardly in his. The gesture seemed unnatural and forced. "It will be alright, Faith," he said gently, his soothing tone comforting to her, despite the awkwardness of his touch. "I'm sure the bishop will see the good it will do all of us."

All of us.

"I see," she said, even though she wasn't certain that was true. She was still reeling from the realization that she had just agreed to join the Amish church, to follow their ways of life as well as worship, and to marry Manuel. For a moment, she felt faint.

"Are you all right, Faith?"

Meekly, she nodded her head. "I'll…I'll be fine, Manuel. Maybe I will take that glass of water, if you don't mind."

After retrieving it, he watched as she sipped at the cool water from their well. "You can change your mind, Faith," he said, his voice shaking just a touch. "Just please tell me before I go speak to the bishop. If I talk to the bishop and he says yes…" He paused and didn't finish the sentence. Immediately, she knew that there would be backlash if she backed out after the bishop was convinced of the benefits to their union.

Determined, she looked up at Manuel and shook her head. "No," she replied. "It's not that. It's just…" She didn't know how to say what she was feeling. In just a few short minutes, she had volunteered to change everything about her life. And all of it felt right and good, the path that God wanted her to travel, with the exception of one thing: Manuel as her husband. "It's a bit overwhelming, is all," she managed to say.

He nodded his head, as if he understood, and spoke no more on the matter. Instead, he retreated outside, leaving her alone to her reflections as he surely needed time to sort his own.

Chapter Eight

"I just don't understand," her mother said, sitting down at the kitchen table. Her face was pale and her eyes wide in complete disbelief at what her only child had just announced. "Why are you doing this? Do you love him?"

Her father scoffed and stood up, pacing the floor. "Love?" he said sharply to his wife. "How could she love him? She doesn't even know him!"

Faith stood before her parents, her hands folded behind her back. She didn't know how to respond. They had reacted exactly as she had expected: shocked and confused.

Faith lifted her chin and summoned the strength to answer her mother. "No, I don't."

Her father shook his head. "See?"

"But I could," Faith said slowly.

"Oh Faith," her mother said, tears starting to form in her eyes. "And to become baptized as an Amish woman? Do you know what that means?"

She nodded her head, understanding only too well what it meant. "Yes, I do. I've met with the bishop."

"This is ridiculous," her father snapped. "I forbid you to do this!"

"John," her mother interfered softly, trying to calm her husband down.

Faith looked at her father, meeting his angry gaze. She had known that her parents would not react favorably but she also knew what she had to do. God had led her to this and she was going to do His will. "Dad, it's not ridiculous. You have to have faith in me...faith that I know what I'm doing."

"What about your job? Your career?"

She smiled softly. "I think raising six children is just as worthy a vocation, don't you?" Although it hadn't been Faith's intention, she realized the double meaning behind her own words. Had not her own mother wished for more children to do exactly what Faith was now doing? Staying home to raise a family full of life and love?

Recognizing the pained look on his wife's face, her father exhaled and tried to comfort her by reaching out to touch her shoulder, a gesture of understanding and support. Lifting his eyes to stare at his daughter, he sighed. "You've made up your mind, haven't you?" When she nodded her head slowly, her father placed his hand on his forehead as though he had a headache. Indeed, Faith wondered if her announcement pained him that much. "Truly, we cannot talk you out of this?"

She shook her head.

Her mother fought back her tears, her fingers pulling at the edges of the tissue in her hand. "I had hoped for something more for you, Faith," she said slowly. "A marriage of love, not convenience."

"Convenience for him!" her father snapped.

"Dad," Faith started. "It was my idea, not his. I won't have you thinking poorly of Manuel." She paused before she added, "Remember that he saved my life once. Now it is my turn to save his."

She spent the rest of the morning gathering the few things that she needed, things that she hadn't already packed when she had moved into Manuel's house to take care of the children while he was sick. But as she looked around her room, she realized that there wasn't really much that she would need. The bishop had reluctantly agreed to work with Faith privately since she had missed the summer instructional at church. The baptism would take place in October with the other youths who were joining the church that year. But the bishop had been adamant about one thing: she had to immediately begin her life as an Amish woman and, with that, she would leave behind the world of the Englische. She had eight weeks before the baptism and a lot to learn during that time frame.

It was slightly before noon when the buggy pulled into the driveway. Faith's parents stared out the window, looking in disbelief as they watched Manuel slide open the door and step out, pausing to tie the horse to a ring on the side of the barn. Faith felt her own heart begin to beat hard in her chest as she realized that she was actually doing this...leaving home and leaving her family.

It felt surreal when Manuel stopped at the kitchen door, pausing to knock on the metal edge of the screen door. She noticed that her parents didn't move from where they stood. Frowning, she hurried to the door and opened it, forcing a smile at Manuel as she stepped back.

"You ready then?" he said, his own voice soft. His blue eyes stared at her and he looked nervous.

She glanced over her shoulder. "You should say something to my parents," she whispered.

"Ah," he replied, taking a deep breath as he reached for his straw hat and removed it from his head. He cleared his throat as he stepped through the door. "Alright, then."

Over the years, Faith's parents had met Manuel Petersheim on more than one occasion, at farm auctions, at Rebecca's wedding, at the local stores, and most recently at

Rebecca's funeral. Since the Amish tended to be private and withdrawn from the Englische world, there had not been too many interactions. Despite living next to the Amish, Faith's parents had clung more to their Mennonite friends and family. And they certainly had never expected to find Manuel standing in their kitchen, hat in hand, greeting them as his future in-laws.

"Right gut to see you again," he managed to say.

Faith's father stared at Manuel, his face devoid of emotion.

"I'm sure Faith told you what her intentions are," Manuel said, standing beside her and glancing at her. For a moment, there was a look of relief on his face when she met his eyes. "I'm honored that she's willing to do this."

"Wish I felt the same," John replied sharply. "I think you are both foolish and rushing into this."

"John," his wife said, laying her hand on his arm.

"I'll have my say," her father snapped. "She's not just getting married, Marie. She's changing her entire lifestyle!"

Faith lowered her eyes, wishing that she could disappear. She wanted to get on with her life, the new life that she had chosen, a life that would honor Rebecca and a life that would be surrounded by the love of six children. Yet, she knew that she had to stand there and let her parents express themselves. It, too, was the honorable thing to do.

To her surprise, Manuel spoke up to her father. "She's joining a family, a family that loves, needs her and welcomes her."

Faith looked up, surprised by his choice of words. A family that loves her? While she knew he meant the children, she wondered if he were including himself in that equation.

And, to her further surprise, she realized that she secretly found the idea pleasant. Deep down, she realized that she hoped that he did, even if it wasn't the type of romantic love that most marriages were built upon. But, perhaps, it could grow into the type of love that formed a good, strong partnership and friendship.

When they finally left her parents' farm, Faith felt as if she might faint. Her head was light and fuzzy, her heart pounding inside of her chest. She had never lived anywhere else, never known anything but life with her parents. Despite being twenty-nine, she had always known that she would stay with her parents and, eventually, inherit the farm. She had never thought she'd leave and certainly not like this.

He helped her into the buggy before he climbed up beside her, the buggy jiggling under his weight. Taking the reins in his hands, he glanced at her and tried to smile. "Ready then, Faith?" he asked before he backed up the buggy and headed down the driveway.

Silence.

She listened to the silence, broken only by the rattling of the metal wheels and the horse's hooves striking the macadam. It wasn't the first time that she had ridden in a buggy. No, over the years, she had done it many times with Rebecca and her older brothers. The last time, however, had been at Rebecca's funeral. Now, she was seated next to Rebecca's husband, the very man she had promised to marry and spend the rest of her life with.

"You alright, Faith?"

His voice startled her from her thoughts. *Good question*, she thought. "Where are you taking me?"

"My sister's house," he said.

"Which one?" She knew that he came from a large family. She had met all of his siblings over the years.

"Lydia agreed to have you stay with her and her family until the..." He paused, unable to say the word. "Until November."

"I don't understand why I can't stay with the children," she asked.

"Not proper to be living in the house when we aren't married," he explained.

"So how am I to get to the farm to take care of the children?"

He lifted his hands up, showing her the leather reins as an explanation. "Or you could walk. It's only two miles or so," he said.

Faith sighed and leaned back against the seat, staring outside. They passed the farm where Rebecca had grown up and Faith could see the colorful clothing hanging from the line that stretched from the corner of the house to the barn. James was living there now, taking care of the farm. His parents had moved into the grossdaadihaus years ago, a transition that was all too common among the Amish. Parents were rarely put into nursing homes. Instead, they lived with their children in a smaller, separate section of the house.

"Why can't I stay in the grossdaadihaus at your farm?" she asked.

He glanced at her and shook his head. "Faith, it's best if you don't question things so much," he chided her gently. "It will be good for you to lean on Lydia. She'll help you with many things, ja?"

"For eight weeks?" She barely knew Lydia. Living with an entire family for two months would be excruciatingly difficult. Not for the first time, Faith wondered why she was actually doing this. She began to feel that familiar pounding inside of her chest, the beginning of what she knew was a panic attack. But she had given her word...to Manuel, to the children, and to the bishop. She knew that she couldn't back out of this.

"It will go quickly," he said. "You'll see."

When they pulled up to Lydia's farm, Faith felt another moment of panic. It was a farm she had seen many times before that day. With a large red barn and pristine house, it had always been a pretty farm that she noticed when she was driving home from work. For all those years, she had passed this house but never actually knew that Rebecca's sister-in-law lived in it. Now, Faith was going to live there and, one day soon, Lydia would be her own sister-in-law.

"*Wilkom,*" Lydia said, a smile on her face as she opened the kitchen door with her bare foot, welcoming her future sister-in-law with genuine happiness. "Been expecting you."

Faith didn't respond as she walked into the house behind Manuel. It was dark and cool in the kitchen, despite it being a warm summer afternoon.

"Manuel, you can show Faith upstairs, ja? Last room in the back," Lydia said, pointing toward the stairs. "It's small, Faith, but it's private. Had to shuffle my oldest dochder with her younger sisters," she explained.

"Oh!" Faith looked at Lydia then at Manuel. "I'm sorry. I don't want to inconvenience anyone."

"Bah," Lydia said, waving her hand. "No bother at all."

Manuel picked up Faith's small bag and began to walk up the stairs, pausing as he waited for Faith to follow. Once upstairs, he led her down a long, narrow hallway toward a door at the very end of it. "Reckon she means this one," he said.

He turned the doorknob and pushed the door open.

Peering inside, Faith was surprised at how similar it looked to the rooms at Manuel's farm. The walls were painted a simple, pale blue. There was one window with a plain, green shade that covered the top half of the windowpanes. A twin size bed with a faded quilt was pushed against the wall. There was a small nightstand next to it, a kerosene lantern the only thing on it. She noticed that there was no closet, just pegs hanging on the walls and a tall, narrow dresser. That was it. Plain. Simple. Amish.

Manuel set her bag down on the bed and stepped out of the room. He paused for a moment, hesitating as if he wanted to say something to her. She waited, expectantly. But he changed his mind and, lowering his head, walked down the hallway. She heard him as he climbed down the stairs, his footsteps heavy as if he had a large burden on his shoulders. It dawned on her that, perhaps, he was regretting having agreed to this arrangement. Perhaps she was not the only one with doubts.

She had very little to unpack. Her hairbrush, her Bible, and her undergarments. She knew that Lydia would help her make some proper Amish dresses. Certainly that would be their first order of business. The bishop had been rather adamant that, if she was serious about taking the kneeling vow and marrying Manuel, she had to begin living as if she already had.

Back downstairs, she was surprised to see that Manuel was no longer there. She glanced out of the window and saw that his buggy was gone, too. For a moment, she felt abandoned and alone, resenting that he hadn't even said goodbye to her. But, as quick as the thought was there, she shoved it into the dark recesses of her mind. She had to transform her way of thinking. If she had learned one thing from Rebecca it was that demonstrations of affection or even emotion were few and far between when it came to the Amish way of life.

Lydia tilted her head and watched Faith's reaction, giving her a moment of reflection. When Faith realized that Lydia was watching her, she flushed and looked away.

"He'll be back," she said, smiling as if she had a secret. "If that's what you're worried about."

"I should thank you for taking me in," Faith said, changing the subject.

Lydia studied Faith, her eyes taking in the woman standing before her. "Ja vell, seems we have quite the challenge, don't we now? Turn you into a right proper Amish woman in just eight weeks!" She laughed. "Manuel certainly knows how to keep life interesting, ain't so?"

"How's that?" Faith asked, worried that Lydia was laughing at her.

"He couldn't just get remarried, ja? He had to pick an Englische woman at that!"

Faith clenched her jaw, wishing she could speak her mind. She wished that she could tell Lydia that he hadn't picked her. She wasn't a product on a shelf, waiting to be selected. Indeed, it was Rebecca who had selected her. It was the children who had selected her. It was God Himself that had guided her. And it was Faith who had made the offer. "It's not like that," she whispered, trying to hold her tongue.

Lydia smiled. But there was no malice in her expression. "Oh I know that, Faith," she said gently. "We knew he'd get married again. He had no choice, really."

No choice?

Lydia continued. "Those kinner need a mamm, for sure and certain. And, frankly, I'm not displeased that it's you."

This surprised Faith and she met Lydia's gaze. "How is that?" she asked.

"Vell," Lydia said, gesturing to the table as an indication that Faith should sit down. "You were always Rebecca's best friend, you've known her for what? Twenty-five years? That's a lot of history and love to bring to those kinner. And remember something," Lydia added as she moved over to the refrigerator, pulling out a large glass pitcher filled with meadow tea. She poured a glass and set it down before Faith. "I was there, Faith. I heard what she said to you. Rebecca wanted this for Manuel, for her kinner, but also for you."

You help Manny.

Faith lowered her eyes and nodded. That was exactly how she felt, too. Rebecca had wanted this for all of them. She often felt as if the hand of God had been guiding her and, in her mind, she saw Rebecca beside Him, whispering in His ear and pointing down from heaven, her finger identifying Faith as the one that she had chosen for her family.

"He doesn't love me," Faith said, surprised that she had spoken those words out loud.

Lydia raised an eyebrow, peering at Faith from behind her glasses. "Do you want him to?"

Faith paused, thinking about the question. Did she? Did she want him to love her? After all, they both knew that this was a marriage of convenience, a marriage to raise those children and honor Rebecca. She hadn't thought much about what their arrangement would be after the wedding. "I would like that, yes," she said.

"Do you love him?"

"No," she admitted slowly, wishing she felt as confident about it as she wanted to sound. "But I will. I'm sure of it."

Lydia nodded. "There are many different types of love, aren't there?" She didn't wait for Faith to respond. "But what holds a marriage together is the love of God. And that is what is most important."

It was her first lesson, Faith realized. God first, family second. Oh, she had been raised in a God-fearing home. She had gone to church every Sunday, neatly groomed and eager for the children's time at the front of the Mennonite church, sitting on the steps while the pastor spoke about Jesus and God, love and faith. But her family hadn't been very conservative, not like some of the other Mennonites in Lancaster County. Her mother didn't wear a head covering, although Faith remembered that her grandmother always wore one. There was even a whisper that, several generations back, one of her ancestors had been Amish before leaving the church, rather than take the kneeling vow and break it.

"Now," Lydia said. "I reckon it's time to make some proper dresses for you, then." She smiled and walked over to the counter, picking up a brown paper bag. "Manuel brought some fabric from the dry goods store. With both of us working together, we should have you dressed by suppertime!"

Faith hadn't noticed the paper bag on the counter. When Lydia handed it to her, Faith peeked inside, frowning when she saw folded fabric in different colors: blue, green, black, and burgundy. Manuel had bought that for her? "That was awfully thoughtful of him," she said, her voice barely a whisper.

There was an odd look in Lydia's eye as she watched Faith's reaction. "He's always been a gentle soul," she said. "Thoughtful and kind in all ways. He was a right gut older bruder, for sure and certain."

Just one more thing I never knew about him, Faith scolded herself. During the years that he was married to Rebecca, she had never bothered to get to know Manuel. He had always intimidated her, the memory of him saving her always too close to the surface to let her release her shyness. During the months after Rebecca's death when Faith had been helping with the children, she hadn't bothered to break through his tough exterior that still bore the scars of mourning. Yet now, she thought as she ran her hands over the fabric, she was learning more about this man, this man who had loved her best friend and this man she had promised to marry so that she could honor her best friend's dying wish.

"Ja vell," Lydia said. "Best get started then, before the kinner get home from school. Won't get much sewing done then."

For the rest of the afternoon, Lydia and Faith worked with the fabric. It amazed Faith how quickly Lydia worked, her hands so expertly cutting the material and pinning the pieces together before using the sewing machine to create the dresses. Faith watched her hands move, wondering how she would ever learn to do the same. Her own clothes had been store-bought, mostly simple dresses. But her mother had never made her clothing at home.

"Look, Faith!" Rebecca motioned for her friend to join her in the sunroom that was directly off the kitchen. "I made a new dress!" She was excited and held up a black dress that looked identical to the green one that she was wearing. "Do you like it?"

"It's very severe, don't you think?" Faith admitted as she

touched the fabric. "But it looks well made, Rebecca."

"It's for church. For when I become a baptized member. I'll be needing to wear black dresses on Sunday, then," she explained.

"What's wrong with wearing colors on the Lord's day?" Some of the Amish rules didn't seem to make much sense to Faith.

A simple shrug of the shoulders answered the question. Rebecca didn't know why she needed to wear black but she also never thought to ask for an explanation. "I love sewing," Rebecca said, steering the conversation back to a safe topic. "Don't you wish that you could make your own clothes?" The question was asked out of curiosity about the life of the Englische. She had never understood the concept of buying clothing versus making it from bolts of fabrics.

Faith laughed. "Not everyone is as good a seamstress as you are, Rebecca. I'd probably sew the fabric to my fingers if I tried!"

Rebecca frowned and put her hand on her hip, staring at her friend. "Now Faith," she started and Faith immediately knew that a lecture was headed her way. "How can you possibly take care of your family if you can't sew?"

"I don't intend to make clothes for my own family," Faith replied lightly. "I'm not Amish, Rebecca. Mennonites can buy their own dresses at stores."

That response didn't please Rebecca and she scoffed. "Maybe that's the problem with the world. More of you Englische should spend the time making your own clothes rather than simply buying whatever is available in a store. It's an act of love, you know," she said. "To make clothes for yourself, your husband, and your children."

Faith waved her hand at Rebecca. "I don't have a husband or children so what's the point?"

Rebecca turned back to her dress, holding it up toward the window so that she could look at it in a better light. "You will, Faith. Just you wait."

Faith quickly found out that she had a good friend in Lydia. She was just a few years younger than Manuel but seemed wise beyond her years. She had married before Manuel and Rebecca and already had a daughter who was turning fourteen in a few months. It was her last year at school before she would begin her home studies to complete her education as required by the state. With six other children and, from the looks of it, one on the way, Lydia Esh's house was quite busy in the evenings and on the weekends.

And so, her days began to fall into a busy routine. She awoke around five in the morning to help Lydia prepare for the day. Sometimes she would help milk the cows with Lydia and her husband. Other times, she began to collect the laundry for a pre-breakfast washing. Lydia had seven children with another one on the way. Laundry was a never-ending task.

After breakfast, the children would walk to school. Faith would accompany them since it was en route to the Petersheim farm. It was a long walk and she would arrive shortly before eight-thirty, replacing Anna and giving the girl just enough time to hurry to school. Ruthie was usually still asleep and Faith would stand, just for a short while, in the doorway and watch the baby, her two little arms tossed over her head and her mouth puckered as she sucked away during her light morning dreams.

Manuel did his best to avoid the house while Faith was

there. She noticed that almost right away. He wouldn't take the noon meal in the house, avoiding her gaze and her questions. Instead, she would bring him a basket of food into the barn.

Lydia was quick to explain. "It just would not be proper for Manuel to be in the house alone with you."

"I don't understand," Faith retorted. "He needs to eat. And it's his home."

Lydia smiled gently, an understanding look of wisdom in her eyes. "You aren't married yet. No need for idle tongues to be wagging about what's going on in that house, ja?"

"But it was alright when we were not to be married?"

Lydia turned to Faith and raised an eyebrow but said nothing. That was the moment when Faith understood. Her life was no longer her own. It was now being examined under a microscope, an Amish microscope. Being alone in the house could lead to sinful thoughts, which in turn could lead to sinful acts. No need for gossip about the Petersheim family. Surely the community was gossiping anyway, wondering about Manuel's betrothal to Faith, a Mennonite woman who was willingly converting to the Amish faith. It was a very special circumstance, one that permitted Faith the individual instructional with the bishop. Her commitment to the Mennonite faith and her lifelong friendship with the Amish were the only two reasons why he had agreed to permit her this special baptism.

Little by little, Faith realized that Lydia must certainly be correct. She saw almost nothing of Manuel during the week. However, every Friday evening, when it came time for her to walk back down the road to Lydia's, he would pull up to the house in his horse and buggy, waiting patiently for her to emerge from the house with her basket of things. He would stand by the buggy, his straw hat in his hand as if nervous at the prospect of asking her the soon to be familiar question: "May I take you home, Faith?"

At first, she had been confused at the formality of his invitations. By the third week, she found it charming. The way that he waited for her, shuffling his feet and his eyes darting around, looking anywhere but at her, spoke of his respect for her independence to pull out from their agreement. He wasn't taking anything for granted and, for that, she was grateful.

The Friday evening rides back to Lydia's farm quickly became her favorite part of the week. She noticed that he drove slowly, sometimes turning down unnecessary lanes, to take her back to his sister's farm. Quite often, he didn't speak, merely holding the reins and staring out the window. But that didn't bother Faith. She took that time to update him on his children and their progress. Gideon was doing well in math while Benjamin was struggling with reading. Anna and Mary were both strong spellers and Sadie, well, she was a vociferous reader. All of the children were doing excellent in English, a fact that Faith took extra pride in. After school, she was able to help them all with their homework and spent extra time with the younger ones to properly learn their English.

"That's gut," he said one evening. "You have truly taken charge of their education. That has to be the teacher in you."

Faith beamed under his praise. "Oh wouldn't Rebecca be proud?"

Immediately, she sensed that he stiffened. The gay nature of their ride vanished and the muscles in his jaw tensed.

"Manuel," Faith asked softly, placing a hand on his arm. "Why do you get like this when I mention her?"

"She's with God now," was his answer. But that left too

many questions unanswered for Faith.

They rode the rest of the way to Lydia's in silence.

The children's reaction to the announcement about Faith had surprised her. She had expected resentment or tears. After all, she was the "replacement" for their mother. Instead, the children had smiled and seemed to quickly accept Faith as their surrogate mother for the next years of their lives. To them, it was a natural progression. To Faith, it was as though she was having an out of body experience. From being single to being married, from being alone to having six children. It felt surreal to her and she often had to stop herself from what she was doing to pause and reflect on the changes that were soon to come.

In the evenings, Lydia and her husband, John, spent time with Faith after supper, talking about the Ordnung and reading the Bible. Faith also spent a lot of time observing the relationship between Lydia and John. It was a different type of relationship than the one she was familiar with from her own upbringing. Indeed, she became aware at a very early stage that Lydia deferred to John on most decisions. Questions were used instead of mandates. Yet, in most cases, John agreed with Lydia.

One night, Lydia had been crocheting a baby blanket for her sister's new baby when she cleared her throat and looked up at John. "Fannie Zook stopped by today and wondered if our eldest might help with their daughter's new market on Saturdays."

John had looked up from the paper he was reading. "Ja?"

Lydia had nodded. "Ja," she affirmed. "Might be a right nice opportunity to make some extra money over the winter. But mayhaps you think she's too young yet? Too bad we can't try it for a few weeks…" She hadn't finished her sentence, letting the words linger between them.

Faith had watched this exchange, hearing the words that were actually spoken but sensing the underlying concern. This form of communication amazed her for she quickly realized that Lydia was guiding John toward the decision she preferred but she still left the decision in her husband's hands.

"I reckon we might agree for her to try it for a month and see how she makes do," John had finally agreed. "Don't want her sleeping during Sunday service."

Faith found herself learning a lot from these exchanges. It was easy to recognize the respect and reverence that was shared between husband and wife, something that was often misconstrued by the Englisher as an Amish wife being submissive to her husband's will; yet it was becoming obvious to Faith that such exchanges showed a mutual love and devotion that clearly contributed to the strength of the bond in their relationship.

Twice a week, the bishop stopped by the house, visiting to check on Faith's progress. It always worried Faith that she would fail his expectations; especially given that she had no barometer to understand what progress she was to be making. Was it cooking or cleaning? Sewing or knitting? Worshiping or learning Pennsylvania Dutch, a language she highly doubted she would ever be able to speak.

One Sunday, during a non-worship day, Faith was surprised to see a buggy pull into the driveway. The horse was all too familiar: Manuel's. When the doors slid back, the children piled out, Anna the first to get out with Ruthie in her arms. Seeing the baby and the children that she had so grown to love, Faith clapped her hands in delight and, without so much as a word to Lydia, ran out of the house to embrace them.

"Whatever are you doing here?" she asked, touching each child on the cheek. "It's such a long weekend when I don't see you at church!" She scooped Ruthie from Anna's arms and walked back toward the house, children surrounding her. She didn't have to look at Lydia's face to see the approving smile cross her lips. "Did you know about this, Lydia? This wonderful surprise visit?"

"Nee, nee," Lydia professed. "But I'm glad to see your joy and theirs! Wilkom!"

Manuel entered the kitchen last. He was carrying a wrapped package. He seemed unnerved by the noise in the kitchen, not just from his children clamoring around Faith but also from Lydia's children. For a few moments, he stood in the doorway, shuffling his feet as his blue eyes darted around the room, avoiding Faith's gaze.

Recognizing his nervousness, Faith finally handed Ruthie back to Anna and approached Manuel. "*Wie gehts?*" she asked, one of the few phrases in Pennsylvania Dutch that she could use properly and practically without the trace of an Englische accent.

"Mayhaps we could speak on the porch?" he asked, his eyes avoiding hers.

For a moment, her heart flipped inside of her chest and a wave of fear flooded through her. Had he changed his mind? Was he here to deliver bad news? Would she be separated from those children for good? Was this the reason why he had brought them here to visit? To say their goodbyes? She glanced at Lydia who merely shrugged her shoulders and motioned for Faith to follow Manuel. Obediently, she did, walking behind him through the kitchen door and onto the porch.

"Manuel?" she asked, feeling a wave of panic overtake her. She suddenly realized how important the Petersheim family was to her. The thought of not being the mother to Ruthie as well as the others kinner made her queasy. *Please God*, she prayed. *Don't let him change his mind, if not for me, then for the children's sake.*

"I bought this for you," he said, awkwardly thrusting the package at her. "I thought it might be helpful."

Curious, she glanced first at him before turning her attention to the plain brown wrapped package. It was heavy and fairly large. It certainly wasn't more fabric for dresses. "What is this?"

He tried to hide his smile. "Open it and see."

And she did.

The brown paper made a heavy crinkling noise as she peeled it away. He reached for it, helping her in the effort of unwrapping the gift. She handed it to him, feeling a warmth race through her veins when his hand brushed lightly against hers. Another glance at his face and she saw that, indeed, he was proud of this gift that he had bought for her.

Inside were two brown leather books, large and heavy. She turned them over to see what they were: The Ausbund, the hymnal of the Amish. For a moment, she frowned. Lydia had the Ausbund at the house and so did he. Why would she need her own copy? But then, as she opened the cover and peered inside, she saw the reason.

"I..I thought this might help you," he said, leaning over her shoulder to point to a passage. "Being in both German and English."

She lifted her eyes and stared at him. She was speechless.

"I saw you in church last week, following the words in The Ausbund," he explained quietly, taking a step back from her. "And Lydia told me that you were asking her for translations afterward. I rode down to Gordonville yesterday to pick up those books at the bookstore."

She looked back at the books in her hands, tracing the gold words on the front cover with her finger. Manuel had been watching her in church? She hadn't noticed that, last Sunday. And he had been discussing her with Lydia? When had he found the time? The microscope of her new life. Yet, in doing so, he had taken time out of his busy day to journey almost ten miles away and buy her a gift? And such a thoughtful one as this?

"Danke, Manuel," she managed to say, finding it hard to not express what she was truly feeling. She wanted to hug him. She wanted to press her lips against his cheek. She wanted to cry at the magnitude of the gift.

But she didn't.

He nodded his head, pleased with the sincerity of her response. Her simple response, plain and to the point. "Gut," he said, smiling just a touch. "And, if you'd like, I can help you with the German when we are..." He hesitated, just long enough for Faith to realize that, despite this wonderful gift, he was still apprehensive about their arrangement. "Married."

And with those words, she now realized how much she could love this man.

Chapter Nine

The baptism service took place at the Fischer's farm, just a few miles down the road. Despite the weather, the service was being held in the barn since there would be more people attending than usual. Faith was not the only person joining the church on this day. For those that were taking the kneeling vow, baptism was a day of celebration as well as one of reflection. Often times, family members came from other districts to share in the glory of the day.

The congregation was gathered for the service. The men were on one side of the room and the women on the other. For the first forty minutes, the congregation engaged in singing hymns, the songs sang a capella in German. Each song was long and drawn out, the sound eerily comforting on such a gray day. It wasn't until the second hour that the bishop requested the baptismal candidates to come forward and sit in the front of the gathering, men on one bench and the women on the other.

The room was crowded and hot, despite the cool October weather outside. The glow from the kerosene lanterns cast soft flickers of light throughout the barn. The sweet smell of hay filled the air, a scent that Faith found comforting. For a moment, she closed her eyes and silently prayed to God to give her the strength to follow the ways of the Amish and to please Him in doing so. When she finished, she opened her eyes and looked around the room. Immediately, she noticed that Manuel had been watching her, the hint of a proud smile on his lips and his eyes sparkling in the dim light of the room.

When the bishop cleared his throat to begin the baptism

sermon, the candidates bowed their heads and covered their faces in a sign of humility, kneeling before him. The bishop spoke to the congregation, talking about Paul baptizing an Ethiopian. It was the same sermon that had been given to many generations before and would be administered to many generations yet to come, those that followed these particular candidates for baptism. Yet, for all of the people kneeling before him, the words were especially poignant and powerful on this dreary, grey day.

"In Matthew 6, the Savior says that no one can serve two masters. Either he will hate the one and love the other, or he will hold to the one and despite the other. You are now asked if you are willing to renounce Satan and all of his followers, the dark kingdom filled with deceitful and worldly riches," he said as he stood before the baptism candidates. "To renounce your own carnal and selfish will, lusts and affections. In doing so, you pledge yourself to be faithful to God, to receive the Savior Jesus Christ, and to allow yourself to live a life that is led by the Holy Spirit in all obedience to the truth and to remain in this unto death?" He paused before he added a simple question, "Can you acknowledge this with yes?"

Faith listened to the words spoken by the bishop in High German. She had practiced them repeatedly for the past few weeks with Lydia so that she would understand everything that was being said. Even Manuel had come to visit one evening after supper.

That night, Faith had been surprised to see him and, as usual, had that moment of panic that, perhaps, he had changed his mind. Yet, he sat beside her on the sofa, talking with Lydia and her husband until it was time for them to retire.

When they were finally alone in the kitchen, Manuel had

seemed nervous, rubbing his hands along his pants as if drying them of water. At that moment, she had realized that he was sweating.

"You are nervous?" she had asked.

"Ja," he had admitted.

"Of marrying me?" she had ventured, gathering courage from an unknown source.

A strange look had flickered across his face and he shook his head. "Nee, Faith," he had said. "Not of that. I am nervous about your baptism."

That had surprised her. "My baptism?"

He had nodded. "Do you know all of the words and what they mean? Do you want to practice them together, mayhaps?"

She had wanted to smile, to reach out and touch his hand. His offer had moved her and she had realized how very important this was to him. "I think that would be wonderful," she had whispered, hoping that her voice didn't crack from the emotion of the moment.

That evening, for the next hour, he had sat beside her, his arm brushing against hers as they reviewed the small brown book with the words of commitment to the Amish faith. He had helped her understand the High German words that the bishop would speak. He had also patiently worked with her on her responses, gently correcting her pronunciation. Once, when she had mispronounced a word, he had laid his hand atop hers, his fingers stroking her skin gently as he corrected her. Faith had found herself staring at his face as he spoke but not listening to the words. When it had been her turn to say the words again, she had to ask him to repeat himself for she hadn't been paying attention. They had both laughed, too aware of the reason why.

Now, as she knelt before the congregation, she found herself nervous, hoping that she would respond properly and pronounce the words correctly. The last thing she wanted to do was to embarrass Manuel.

After the bishop continued with the rest of the questions concerning baptism, he paused again, his eyes carefully scanning the bowed heads before him. "If you are still intent on taking this baptism," he began, his voice serious and deliberate. "Then I ask you to stay kneeling before me and the congregation. If, however, you have any doubts, this is the time to speak up."

Silence.

When enough time had passed, it was time for each of the candidates to profess their confession of faith. Listening to the other three candidates ahead of her, Faith felt her palms begin to sweat as she tried to repeat in her mind the words that she had practiced for so long. She prayed to God that she would remember them and speak them properly.

"Faith Landes, do you renounce the devil, the world, and your own flesh and blood?"

She nodded her head and whispered, "Ja." Goodbye past life, she thought. Goodbye worldliness. No more cars, no more telephones, no more shopping for clothes. Yet she found that she didn't mind. It was a small price to pay for the reward of those precious children.

"Can you commit yourself to Christ and His church, to abide by it and therein to live and to die?"

She swallowed before she responded with another simple, "Ja."

The bishop took a deep breath before he asked the third and final question, "And in the Ordnung of the church, according to the Word of the Lord, to be obedient and submissive to it and to help therein?"

This was the one that Faith knew she would struggle with for the rest of her life. If she broke this vow, she risked being shunned. Yet she worried constantly that something she might say or do would be against the Ordnung, those unwritten rules that governed the Amish community. Still, despite her trepidation, she said, "Ja," and prayed that God would help her keep that vow.

"Please speak your confession of faith, Faith Landes," the bishop said.

Please, please, please, she prayed. "Ich glaub dab Jesus Christus Gottes Sohn ist," she managed to say, her heart pounded as she professed that she believed that Jesus Christ was, indeed, the Son of God. Once the words escaped her lips, she wanted to breath a sigh of relief but held her breath for she felt the bishop's hands on her head.

"Faith Landes," the bishop said as the deacon poured water on her bare head. "Upon your confessed faith, you are baptized in the name of the Father and the Son and the Holy Spirit, Amen. Whoever believes and is baptized shall be saved." He removed her hands from her face and helped her stand before the congregation. His wife stepped forward and gave her a kiss, the signed of the completion of baptism, before reminding her to be a faithful member of the church.

And with that, her kneeling vow was over and Faith rose to her feet a true Amish woman.

There were very few words from people after the service. She was expected to quickly slip into her role of helping to prepare the fellowship meal, although Lydia paused to give her an approving smile as she squeezed Faith's hand in silent acknowledgement of her baptism. But just as quickly as the exchange happened, the two women were back at work, helping the other women set up the tables for the congregation to share the fellowship meal.

It was after the first seating, while Faith found herself standing alone for a moment, watching the younger women prepare the tables for the next group of church members, that Manuel approached her, his hands in his pockets and a glow about his face. He glanced around to make certain no one was watching before he reached out and slipped something into her hand. "Something to remember today by, ja?" he said with a timid smile just before he hurried back to where the men were standing.

She stared after him, stunned by the gesture. Was this his way of letting her know that he was proud of her? That she had pleased him with how hard she had practiced and how well she had managed to repeat the commitment vows? Her eyes fell to the small package in her hand. It was wrapped in simple brown paper with a string holding it together. Glancing back at him one last time, she noticed that his eyes were upon hers, watching her from where he stood with his peers.

Looking back toward the package, she pulled at the string and pushed back the paper. Inside was a neatly folded and pressed white handkerchief, embroidered on one corner with purple lilacs. The edges were stitched with white lace in a scalloped pattern. It was beautiful, a gift to be treasured, just as much for its fine craftsmanship as for the humbled manner with which it had been given to her. She held the handkerchief in her hand and lifted her eyes to seek Manuel's. When she saw him still watching her, she smiled and bowed her head, a silent way of thanking him for his thoughtful, not to mention touching, gift.

"We're going to have a supper at the house after my baptism," Rebecca said to Faith as they stood in the kitchen making cookies. "I asked Mamm if you could come and she said that you should."

Faith didn't know how to respond. She was despondent over Rebecca's decision to take the kneeling vow, suspecting that this new, serious Rebecca was not going away anytime soon. Her friend had changed, matured in a way that created a distance between them at times.

"You'll come, ja?"

Nodding her head, Faith forced a smile. "I wouldn't miss it for the world," she had said.

Rebecca hugged her, a rare embrace that startled Faith. Like most Amish people, Rebecca was not very demonstrative with signs of affection. "I knew you would," she beamed. "It just wouldn't be the same without you!"

The admission had warmed Faith's heart and she smiled as she said, "Too bad I can't attend the service."

"I wish you could, too. If only you were Amish..." she lamented and, to Faith's surprise, she saw the serious look on Rebecca's face. "Wouldn't that be just perfect?"

It was later that afternoon, back at Lydia's house, that Manuel asked Faith if she'd like to go for a buggy ride with him. She felt shy, a new nervousness about her, when she was in his presence but she welcomed the time alone with him. Buggy rides, she knew, were an accepted form of courtship with the

Amish. Unmarried couples could be alone in a buggy without risk of wagging tongues speculating about their virtue.

At first, Manuel drove the horse in silence, his eyes on the road ahead. She glanced at him, wondering what was on his mind and waiting for him to speak. In the silence, she listened to the rattling of the buggy as the horse pulled it along the road, the sound soothing her frayed nerves.

"They'll be announcing our wedding at the next service," he finally said, a nervous look in her direction.

She had known that already but didn't say so. "Oh?"

He nodded his head. "Lydia has offered to host the ceremony and I'll start inviting people then. I reckon you have some family and friends you'd like to invite, then?"

"My parents, I suppose," she replied, hesitating before she added, "But I don't want to invite anyone from my old life." It was too complicated, she pondered, to invite colleagues from her work or friends that she had made during her college years. She wanted a fresh start in her new life as the wife of an Amish man. "Is that horrible?"

For a moment, he contemplated what she had asked. She could see him reflecting upon it, spending time mulling over his answer. "Nee," he answered solemnly. "I understand. It's a new life for you. Bringing the old life into it seems to bring conflict at a time you are seeking peace."

A wave of relief washed over her. She had been concerned that he would think she was ashamed. That wasn't the case at all. It would take her time to adapt to the ways of the Amish, both culturally and religiously. She needed that time before she would be able to balance both worlds simultaneously. "Yes," Faith said with a soft sigh. "That's it exactly."

They rode in silence again, Faith settling back into the velvet seat as she listened to the soothing noise of the horse's hooves and the gentle humming of the buggy wheels. It was still a novelty to her, riding in a buggy. She hoped that she'd never get tired of it and that she would always find it magical.

"I want to tell you," Manuel said at last. "That I'm in awe of what you have done."

Awe? Faith repeated the word in her head and wondered what he meant. That was a strong word, a word that hinted at pride. She wondered what the bishop would think about that.

"You have renounced the world and committed yourself to obey the Ordnung for my children," he continued.

She placed a hand on his arm, politely interrupting him. "I have accepted Jesus as the Son of God and as my savior, Manuel. From that, everything else stems."

He nodded his head, appreciating her words. "Ja, I agree."

"That is for my own salvation just as much as for your family's," she added.

Manuel looked at her and smiled. His eyes sparkled and looked alive, his own, quiet reverence to the Amish faith and her newfound commitment to it apparent in the way that he responded to what she had just expressed. "Well said, Faith. You make me very happy with that."

They rode the rest of the way back to Lydia's farm in silence, a comfortable silence between two people who had found a common ground on which to build their future relationship, one that centered on God just as much as it centered on each other.

Chapter Ten

She stood in the back of the room, the handkerchief with the embroidered lilacs clutched in her hands. There was a sea of people crowding into the house, the men in their Sunday suits and the women wearing green, burgundy, and pink dresses. But only one person wore blue: Faith.

Over the past three months, she had attended church services with Lydia every other Sunday. Faith found the singing during the service to be mesmerizing, so beautiful and uplifting, despite not understanding what was being sung. After church service, Faith would hurry home to Lydia's house and disappear upstairs where she sat on the edge of the bed, reading through her Ausbund, the special one that Manuel had bought for her, one that was in both German and English. For the next hour, Faith would read through the three songs that had been sung at church, reading the German words before she read the translation. She could shut her eyes and hear the singing in her ears, the lifting up of voices praising God. And her heart would swell with love and happiness.

Yet today was different. Today was a Thursday, the last Thursday in November. Today she would attend a church service but it would be a different kind of service for, at the end of it, she would become Manuel's wife. No, she corrected herself. She would forever be known as Manuel's Faith.

Lydia had helped her make the traditional light blue dress for the ceremony. For that, Faith was grateful. She had been nervous, her hands shaking whenever she had tried to hold the needle or cut the material. Sensing Faith's raw nerves and anxiety, Lydia had quickly taken charge of the process.

To make matters worse, she hadn't seen much of Manuel over the past four weeks. During the week, when Faith arrived at the farm to help with the housekeeping and tend to the baby while the children were at school, Manuel had usually been outside working. She almost had thought that he was avoiding her. Once Anna and the other kinner arrived home from school, Faith immediately felt better, helping them with their afternoon chores. By five in the afternoon, she would head back to Lydia's farm, walking the two miles, a time of solace that helped her clear her head.

But she still couldn't help wonder about Manuel's strange behavior. On a Saturday, when Faith and Lydia sat mending some clothing, Faith had gathered the courage to mention her concerns to his sister.

Lydia had tried to explain to her that Manuel was only doing the proper thing: giving her space. Now that the community knew that Faith had joined the church and would marry Manuel, it wouldn't be appropriate for him to be alone in the house with her, even more so than before. Tongues would wag and speculation might start about the extent of their relationship and the real reason for the wedding.

"Faith?" Lydia called up the stairs. "You should get down here to eat something."

Food? Faith blanched at the thought. Her stomach was in a turmoil. How could she possibly hold down any food when, in just a few short hours, she would be committing herself to love, honor, and obey a man that she barely knew, a man that she had hardly spoken two full sentences to during the past month? Oh, she had caught him watching her as he worked in the barn. On the days that she did the laundry while the children were at school, she noticed that he would stand in the shadows of the barn, his face turned in her direction as she hung the wet clothing on the line. But not once did he come to her, to greet her or share the noon meal with her. For that, Faith had been left on her own with baby Ruthie.

Still, she hadn't minded. The time that she spent alone with the baby had been joyful. Without doubt, Ruthie was a happy baby, completely unaware of the pain that her life had brought upon the Petersheim family. Faith found that her relationship with the infant only grew closer with each passing day. Ruthie's smiles and giggles, the way the baby tried to pull at her hair or at the strings of her prayer kapp, only furthered the adoration that Faith felt for her. She doubted that she could love another human being as much as she loved that baby, for the two of them seemed to be left on their own, needing the mutual love that they felt for each other.

"Ja, vell," Lydia said as she appraised Faith. "I'd say you look right gut for your wedding day."

Faith felt her stomach twist at the words. *Wedding day? What am I doing*, she asked herself, not for the first time.

With Faith staying at Lydia's house, the church service and ceremony would be held there. During the previous week, Faith had helped clean the downstairs, washing windows and floorboards before hurrying to Manuel's in the afternoon to tend to his house, the laundry, and the children. Each night, she was exhausted and secretly wished that Manuel would offer to drive her home to Lydia's. Yet, she hadn't even seen him during those days.

Disappointment began to fill her mind as she looked toward the barn in the evening, knowing that he was in there, before she began the thirty-minute walk back to Lydia's farm.

So, when she heard the buggies starting to pull into Lydia's driveway on the Thursday morning, Faith felt her heart pounding even harder, worried that Manuel wouldn't show up but also panicking that he would. The conflict in emotions made her edgy and distracted as she helped to set up the benches in the large gathering room while Lydia's younger children set worn copies of the Ausbund upon each seat. As other people began to arrive, Faith realized that the day was not much different than any church Sunday. There were no flowers, no candles, no gifts, and no hugs. Instead, a simple handshake and, when the women had arrived, the friendly kiss of sisterhood as they greeted each other.

In her lifetime, Faith had attended many different weddings. Friends from her college years had invited her to theirs, mostly held at Presbyterian or Catholic churches. Cousins had been married at the Mennonite church. And, of course, she had been invited to Rebecca's wedding, one of the three Amish weddings she had ever attended. At the time, she hadn't paid much attention to anything but to how radiant her friend looked. After all, Faith hadn't been able to understand the sermon and the songs. This time however, she had studied the words in advance and, even though she wasn't fluent in German or Pennsylvania Dutch by any stretch of the imagination, she had studied the songs that would be sung and the words that would be spoken by the bishop, memorizing their translations as well, so that she would know exactly what was said.

"Faith!"

She turned around at the sound of her name. Anna, Mary, and Sadie ran up to her and greeted her with the familiar handshake. Sadie beamed, a smile on her face that spoke of her pleasure in this day. "Just think," she whispered into Faith's ear while squeezing her hand. "Tonight you'll be coming home with us to stay!"

Another moment of panic set in and Faith forced herself to swallow, hesitating before she responded with a nervous smile, "Imagine that, Sadie! How fortunate am I!"

"Daed has Ruthie," Anna said. "I told him I'd take her but he said he'd ask Lydia."

Faith nodded. "That's right smart of him, Anna. That way you won't be interrupted during the service." She was grateful for the distraction, her palms sweating as she realized that, indeed, not only would she be returning to the Petersheim's farm that evening, but also it would be her home forevermore. She would live there for the rest of her life, perhaps one day moving to the smaller grossdaadihaus when the children would be older and one of them would take over the farm.

Her heart began to palpitate inside of her chest. When that happened, she'd be living alone with Manuel. Without young children, it would just be the two of them. For a moment, panic returned. What would they do when it was just the two of them, she wondered. A voice inside of her head stopped her, reminding her that such a time was a long way in the future. Plenty of time to know Manuel, she told herself.

Glancing around the room, she caught sight of Manuel speaking with Lydia just outside of the doorway leading to the porch. As always, he looked handsome in his black suit and vest. Even more becoming was how he was holding Ruthie, a genuine smile on his face. Indeed, true to Anna's word, he was handing Ruthie to Lydia, pausing just momentarily to tickle the baby under her chin before he joined the other men.

When I leave here today, she thought, *that man will be my husband.* The thought sent her into a spiral of mixed emotions. The confliction caused her angst and she found herself chewing on her lower lip, questioning herself once again until the image of Rebecca passed through her memory.

"Just think, Faith," Rebecca gushed. "One day, you'll be getting married and Manuel and I will attend your wedding!"

It was just a few days before her wedding to Manuel and Rebecca was giddy with excitement. While Faith could not be one of her attendants on that day since she wasn't Amish, Rebecca had repeatedly told her that she was the attendant of her heart. Together, they had worked on her blue wedding dress, a plain dress that Rebecca would wear over and over again throughout the years. One day, she had told Faith, she would be buried in that dress, a morbid thought that Faith had hated to consider.

But for now, as they helped Rebecca's mamm bake pies for the wedding fellowship, Rebecca was focused more on helping her friend share in the joy, wishing that she, too, would soon get married.

But Faith had other plans. When Rebecca announced her intentions to attend Faith's wedding, she had merely laughed at her friend. "I doubt it," Faith replied, gently nudging her friend's shoulder with her own as both of their hands were covered in flour. "I'll be an old spinster, just you watch!"

"Oh Faith," Rebecca cried, genuinely alarmed. "Don't you say such a horrid thing!"

Again, Faith laughed at the expression on Rebecca's face. "It's not that horrid, truly. I want to teach. My students will be my children. I don't need to get married to have a family and I've never really met anyone who interests me," she said. "Not like the way you light up when you are with Manuel."

"Hmmph!" Rebecca sniffed, feigning disappointment in her friend. "Vell, if that's the case, you will just have to share the family that Manuel and I have. You need your own children and family." She paused and looked over at Faith, a smile forming on her lips. It was clear that she had an idea, an idea that pleased her greatly and gave her peace regarding the dilemma of what to do about Faith and a family. "Ja, that's just what I'll do!"

Faith shook her head, enjoying this light-hearted and joyous Rebecca. "What will you do?"

"Why, if you don't have your own family," Rebecca had said with a smile on her face. "I'll just give you mine!"

It was just like a regular church service with the exception of the high number of people that attended. In addition to Manuel and his family members, both those of the immediate family as well as the extended, other members of the church district and Faith's family were also in attendance. To Faith, many of the faces looked to be the same as those that had attended Rebecca's funeral just six months prior.

As always, the service opened with the congregation joining together to sing a song from the Ausbund. One of the men began by singing the first syllable of the hymn in a long, drawn out singsong manner. The rest of the congregation joined in. Each syllable was sung to a specific tune, one hymn often taking upwards of thirty minutes to be sung.

Faith knew that the bishop was going to present a sermon after the hymn was finished. Then, there would be another hymn and another sermon. At that point, the bishop would ask for Manuel and Faith to come forward for the exchanging of the vows. Faith realized that she knew the process from not just studying the book that Lydia gave to her but also from having attended several of the weddings in the Yoder family, including Rebecca's marriage to the man that would become her own husband in less than two hours.

She didn't know whether to find the situation ironic or tragic. Perhaps both.

She looked up and glanced around the room. Manuel was sitting toward the front, his eyes on the bishop as he sang the Ausbund verse by heart. He looked at peace and calm, not nervous at all. And then, his blue eyes flickered in her direction, catching sight of her watching him. With just a slight movement of his head, he was no longer looking at the bishop but meeting her gaze. There was a moment, just a small moment, when he ceased singing and gave her the smallest hint of a smile. It was just enough to let her know that, indeed, everything was going to be just fine.

By the time that the second sermon was over, it was just after eleven. Faith felt her hands tremble when she saw the bishop stand before the congregation and, clearing his throat, ask for Manuel and Faith to rise and join him at the front. It was time. From deep within her core, Faith found the strength to stand and join Manuel, and both of them stood in front of family, friends, and church members to declare their intentions.

The bishop leveled his gaze at Manuel as he began to enunciate the wedding vows. "Can you confess, brother, that you wish to take this, our fellow-sister as your wedded wife, and not to part from her until death separates you, and that you believe this is from the Lord and that through your faith and prayers you have been able to come this far?"

Manuel tensed at the phrase *until death separates you* but, after a quick recovery, he nodded his head and said, "Ja." Despite the softness of his voice, Faith knew that he was comfortable with this decision.

The bishop turned his attention to Faith. "Can you confess, sister, that you wish to take this, our fellow-brother as your wedded husband, and not to part from him until death separates you, and that you believe this is from the Lord and that through your faith and prayers you have been able to come this far?"

She bit her lip and nodded her head. The word seemed stuck in her throat. But no one spoke until she finally forced out a soft "Ja" in response to the bishop's question.

"Since you, Manuel Petersheim, have confessed that you wish to take our fellow-sister to be your wedded wife, do you promise to be faithful to her and to care for her, even though she may suffer affliction, trouble, sickness, weakness, despair, as is so common among us poor humans, in a manner that befits a Christian and God-fearing husband?"

Once again, Manuel nodded as he enunciated his answer: "Ja."

The bishop returned his gaze to Faith. "And you, Faith Landes, you have also confessed that you wish to take our fellow-brother to be your wedded husband. Do you promise to be faithful to him and to care for him, even though he may suffer affliction, trouble, sickness, weakness, despair, as is so common among us poor humans, in a manner that befits a Christian and God-fearing wife?"

"Ja," she managed to say, feeling as if she were watching the entire scene as a bystander, not a participant. Everything felt surreal and unnatural. *Is this really happening?* she wondered.

The bishop took one step back and, gesturing toward him, he said, "Extend your right hand to each other." When they did so, he covered their hands with his and said, "The God of Abraham, the God of Isaac, and the God of Jacob be with you both and help your family come together and shed His blessing richly upon all of you. Now, go forth as a married couple. Fear God and keep His commandments."

And with that, they were married.

It was later, after the service was formally over, when the newly-married couple sat together at the corner table, that the people who had attended the service began approaching them in pairs to greet them for the first time as husband and wife. Faith knew many of the people but just as many were unknown to her. Manuel introduced her to each couple, explaining where they lived and whom they were related to. By the end of the greeting period, her head was spinning and she couldn't remember the names of anyone. She had stopped counting how many Katies, Sylvias, Lindas, and Amos she had met. The names began to blur together and she found herself barely listening.

Instead, she was looking for the children, wanting to make certain that Benjamin and Sadie had eaten enough. She tried to find Ruthie, curious as to which relative was holding her now.

"Faith?"

She felt his hand on her arm, his touch soft and gentle. Nevertheless, she jumped, startled out of her thoughts.

Pivoting in her seat, she looked at Manuel and tried to meet his eyes. "I'm sorry," she apologized. "Did you say something?"

There was a look of understanding in his expression. His blue eyes studied her face. For the first time, she realized how truly handsome he was, with deep-set eyes and high-cheekbones. Even with his full beard, there was a look of elegance about him, a look that she had never noticed before this morning. Or, rather, a discovery she might very well have noticed but avoided thinking about prior to this moment.

"I wanted to make certain you had enough to eat," he said, his voice faltering. She realized that he, too, was as uncomfortable as she was. He ran his finger along her wrist, just a brief gesture of familiarity that caused her heart to quicken, before he removed his hand. "Don't want you having to cook tonight when we get back home."

Nodding, she glanced back around the room. "I...I was just thinking the same thing. However, I'm more worried about the children." But she didn't see them anywhere. "I hope they had enough to eat."

"They'll be fine," he replied gently. "Don't you worry about them none."

Shifting in the chair, Faith turned to him, meeting his gaze and fighting the urge to get emotional. It was there, inside of her chest: the emotions of the day, the commitment to the future, the memories of the past. They threatened to unleash themselves if she didn't suppress them. "Manuel," she said softly. "What happens next?"

"Ja vell," he said, glancing around the room, leaning closer to her so that she could hear him above the noise in the room. "They'll be some singing before people begin to leave." His eyes drifted to the clock over his sister's sink in the kitchen.

"Most will be leaving by three, four at the latest. Cows still need milking, regardless of the day."

Of course, she thought. The needs of the farm were at the center of most daily routines. She dreaded the thought of leaving Lydia's house, dreaded the idea that she would drive off with Manuel and arrive at the farm, her new home, with a ready-made family. She worried about their expectations from her, especially Manuel. During the summer, she had been able to take charge for she had very little at stake. Now, however, she was a wife and a mother in a world that, despite being familiar to her, made her feel as though she was an outsider.

And *tonight*?

She was nervous about what Manuel expected from her. It was one thing to take care of the children, to marry him in order to fulfill a promise to her friend. But to be a true wife? It was the one thought that had caused her the most grief, causing her to lie awake at night, praying to God for help and guidance. She wasn't ready to be a wife, not in that physical sense, to a man she barely knew, a man that had been married to her best friend, a man that she didn't know if she really loved.

Chapter Eleven

He didn't awaken her when he slipped from beneath the covers. At least not intentionally. In truth, she hadn't slept much during the night. Instead, she had lain beside him in the bed, listening to the sound of his breathing, hearing the gentle rumbling of a soft snore from time to time. Throughout the night, she had fought the urge to cry, not understanding the emotions that she was feeling.

Indeed, as she had expected, it had been a strange feeling when they pulled up to the Petersheim farm. The children had been giddy and laughing, happy that they had a new mamm, one that they already knew and loved. For the children, Faith had always been a part of their lives, although not as active in recent years, that was true. But she was already a part of their family and the fact that their mamm had been her best friend meant that there was a history to be shared.

Manuel, however, had been quiet. He refused to look at Faith and, after helping her down from the buggy, he mumbled something in Pennsylvania Dutch and led the buggy toward the stable to untack the horse.

Confused, Faith had wandered into the house, realizing that this was now *her* home. In all likelihood, she would never live anywhere else. Home, she thought. It was a strange feeling. It still felt like Rebecca's home, not her own.

The children had clamored around her, gracing her with an occasional hug and big smiles. Even Ruthie seemed to know that something was different and she kept waving her arms happily in the air from the high-chair.

"Perhaps Gideon, you and your brother could help your daed," Faith had suggested as she glanced at the clock. "I sure bet he could use a hand with the evening milking."

It was Anna who nodded to the two boys. "You listen to Mamm now," she urged them.

Mamm. The word had struck Faith and she lifted a hand to her chest, feeling her heart pounding. How easily that word had slid from Anna's lips. How easily they had accepted her into their family. For a moment, she wondered why Rebecca was replaced with so little apprehension on the part of the kinner. Why hadn't they fought it? Why had they embraced Faith's presence with such elation?

The pounding inside of her chest never faded that evening. She had been nervous and jumpy, waiting for Manuel and the boys to come inside after tending to the animals. It was dark when they finally stomped into the kitchen, Manuel pausing to hang up his hat from a peg that jutted out from the wall. He glanced at Faith and forced a quick smile before he hurried to the sink and washed his hands. The fact that he was avoiding her gaze was more than apparent.

"Oh," she had said, stepping aside, making room for him at the counter. "You hadn't changed your clothes." She reached for a hand towel, waiting for him to finish washing his hands.

Surprised, Manuel had looked down and realized that, indeed, he had tended the evening chores wearing his black suit. "I didn't, did I?" he said sheepishly. His nice Sunday clothes were splattered with dirt, hay, and manure was lining the hem of his trousers. "Must've slipped my mind." He took the towel that Faith offered him and nodded his appreciation. Then, with a quick glance at the clock, he looked at the kinner. "Reckon you best be going to bed, then," he said, nodding to

Anna to take charge of the younger ones. "Been a long day and you have school tomorrow."

Once the room had quieted down, Faith had stood against the counter, watching Manuel with a mixture of curiosity and apprehension. She didn't know what to do. She was uncertain of how to act. Earlier that day, she had stood before the community, promising to be his wife. Yet, it was the one thing she didn't know how to do. She wished that he would say something to her, anything to help guide her in this new role as a wife. His wife. Instead, he sighed and walked to the bedroom on the first floor. He paused as he stood in the doorway, his back to her. "I moved my things back down here," he said. "Reckon it was time, ja?"

And that had been it.

There had been no hugs, no kisses. There had been no loving embraces. He had merely said that he was going to retire for the night and, behind a closed door, he had changed his clothes and crawled into bed, leaving the kerosene lantern burning on her nightstand.

Realizing that he wasn't coming back to the kitchen, Faith had wandered to the doorway of the bedroom, peering inside with trepidation. The last time she had seen him in this room, the room that he had shared with Rebecca, had been when Ruthie was born. After Rebecca's death, he had slept upstairs, not wanting to sleep in that bedroom, a room full of memories. Now, however, with a new wife, it was time to move back into the master bedroom. Standing in the doorway, Faith had watched Manuel for a moment, wondering how hard that move had actually been.

In the glow emanating from the lantern, Faith had quickly changed out of her blue dress, hanging it on a hanger and placing it on the peg in the wall. The air was chilly and she had quietly slipped on the white nightgown, glancing once over her shoulder at Manuel before turning back to the dresser where she removed the white prayer kapp, setting it down beside her hairbrush before she pulled the bobby pins from her hair. It had cascaded down past her shoulders in loose waves. Once more, she had looked over at Manuel, wondering if he was still awake, wondering if he was waiting for her.

To her relief, she realized that he was not.

She had never known a man. Yet now, as the wife of her best friend's husband, she knew that there would come a day when she would have to be more than a wife in name. However, it was immediately clear that this would not be the night. Her wedding night, she realized, would be spent sleeping and not exploring the unknown world of true marriage. Yes, she realized, she was content with that. She needed more time to come to grips with the thought of eventual intimacy.

Manuel had apparently recognized her apprehension and respected it. Perhaps, she realized, he was having the same thoughts. Regardless, she was relieved that he was leaving her alone to her own reflections, probably working out his own turmoil over the loss of his beloved Rebecca and the *acquisition* of Faith as the unlikely *replacement*. That thought bothered Faith and she had spent most of the night tossing and turning, troubled by the fact that she was considered perhaps just that: a replacement.

So, in the morning, when he slipped out from under the covers, she listened to him shuffle through the darkness. He had slept in simple pajamas and now, she could hear him getting changed into his work clothes. She guessed it was four-thirty although there was no clock in the room to tell her whether or not she was right.

She sat up in the bed, holding the covers against her chest to ward off the morning cold. "Shall I help you, Manuel?"

"Ach," he said, sitting down on the edge of the bed, his weight causing her to move toward him, her leg brushing against his hip. Manuel leaned over toward her, something she sensed more than saw for she could barely make out his silhouette in the darkness. "I didn't mean to wake you, Faith." She felt his hand on her shoulder, gently pushing her back on the mattress. "Stay in bed and sleep some more," he commanded gently. "I'll be back in a few hours. Mayhaps a nice hot breakfast would be right gut then?"

It was something. A small something. A simple gesture that warmed her heart. He had sat next to her. He had touched her shoulder. He had wanted her to stay comfortable and in bed. And he had spoken to her, his gentle words and soft tone caressing her ears. It was more than she had received from him since the day he had saved her life.

She listened as he leaned down and pulled on his work boots before standing up and quietly walking to the door. Once he passed through the door, shutting it behind him, she heard him cough in the kitchen, pausing just for a moment to run the kitchen faucet for, she imagined, a cup of water. A few seconds later, the door to the washroom squeaked open and she heard him walking down the porch, his footsteps gradually fading away.

For the next thirty minutes, she laid in bed, listening to the noise of the clock in the other room. When it chimed five times, she realized that she had been correct about Manuel waking up at four-thirty in the morning. For the past six months, he had been doing that every day, greeting the darkness by himself as he went about his chores. The sun would rise and the sky would shift from blackness to a warm orange. Yet he did it alone, no help or company during those early morning hours.

The thought bothered her and, aware that she wasn't about to fall back to sleep, even after her almost sleepless night, she tossed the covers back and quickly got out of the bed. There was a metal tin of matches hanging from the wall near a strike pad. She had used it before when she had stayed at the house. Striking the match, she turned back to the kerosene lantern and lit it, appreciating the golden glow that instantly lit up the room.

Twenty minutes later, she was dressed and carrying a pot of hot coffee through the chilly morning air as she headed toward the barn. She had put on a black sweater over her dress and covered her head with a cream colored scarf. Even still, it was cold.

She heard him before she saw him. He was talking softly to one of the cows as he attached the mechanical milking machine to her udders. Faith couldn't understand what he said for he was speaking in Pennsylvania Dutch but, from the tone, she knew that he was soothing the animal.

She cleared her throat to let him know that she was there.

The look on his face was one of complete surprise. "Faith?" He stood up, resting his hand on the cow's rump. "Why are you up? It's early."

"Yes," she said. "Yes it is." Then she lifted the coffee pot and two mugs, smiling at him. "I thought I would bring my husband some coffee to warm him up while I kept him company," she said. *Husband.* The word sounded odd coming from her lips. She had to force herself to say it and could barely look him in the eye when she did. *Husband.* Indeed, it didn't sound real at all to call Manuel Petersheim her husband.

Manuel didn't seem to notice. "Why," he started, sounding genuinely pleased, his face lighting up. "That was right thoughtful of you."

She poured coffee into one of the mugs and walked over to hand it to him. As he took the mug, his hand brushed against hers and she blushed. "You like it black, right?" She knew the answer to the question but asked it anyway, hoping that it would break the ice.

"Ja, black," he said, nodding his head. He shut his eyes as he sipped the warm liquid. "Ah, dat ist gut!"

Another small something. A compliment. Despite the trepidation in her heart, Faith was pleased with how the morning was progressing. Manuel seemed to be loosening up, just a little. It gave her hope...hope that a happy future might actually be possible.

"You know," she said slowly, glancing down the aisle of cows waiting to be milked. "I have always helped my father with the milking. I'd get up early so that he wouldn't be doing all that work alone. So, you see, I'm used to it, Manuel." She looked at him, trying to gauge his reaction. "I'd like to help you too."

He leaned against the cow's rump, one hand holding the coffee mug and the other tugging thoughtfully at his beard. His blues eyes stared at her, assessing her. "You would, ja?"

She nodded her head.

"Vell," he said, sipping at the coffee again. "Reckon I could use a hand in the morning. Boys usually get out here about six to start on the stalls and to drop the hay. But if you want to help with milking, that might be right gut." He raised an eyebrow, a conniving smile on his face and added, "That and a pot of hot coffee, of course."

Was he teasing her? She felt her heart flip with joy. In less than an hour, three small blessings from this man, her husband. Signs that everything would be all right. His approval pleased her and she felt like a young schoolgirl, as if the most handsome boy in class was paying attention to her. She flushed and lowered her eyes, hoping that he didn't see her reaction. Yet, when he chuckled, she knew that he had.

They worked in silence for the next hour, Manuel occasionally giving her directions so that she could learn the routine of his morning with the cows and how to use the milking equipment. While it wasn't too different than how her father worked his dairy, there were certain nuances to Manuel's order of business. She listened attentively, nodding her head in understanding and, to both of their pleasure, she picked everything up quickly.

They were just finished with the milking when the two boys wandered into the barn. Manuel glanced at the clock on the wall and raised an eyebrow. It was almost six-thirty. They were half-an-hour late.

"Good evening, boys," he teased. Gideon tried to apologize for oversleeping, but his daed held up his hand. "Just get the stalls cleaned and hay tossed down in a timely manner, son," he said. "Faith..." He hesitated before correcting himself. "Your mamm will have breakfast ready by seven. Don't be tardy then, ja?"

Manuel started to walk back to the house, pausing just long enough for Faith to catch up with him. They walked side-by-side through the breaking light of dawn toward the home, a comfortable silence between them.

Inside, Faith quickly went about the task of preparing the breakfast for the family. *My family*, she corrected. Anna was the first to come down, greeting both Faith and her daed with a big happy smile. Without being asked, she started to set the kitchen table while Faith cooked at the stove. By the time Sadie and Mary emerged from upstairs, Ruthie in Mary's arms, the kitchen was alive with the warm and enticing smell of breakfast. Manuel was sitting at the head of the table, enjoying another cup of hot coffee while perusing through the daily newspaper, which he had picked up while walking with Faith from the barn to the house.

At this moment, Faith felt at peace with herself. She glanced around at the movement of morning, listening to the eggs sizzling in the pan and smelling the toast in the oven. Sadie was standing impatiently before Mary, letting her older sister brush her hair and twist it back over her ears into tiny rolls before pinning it at the nape of her neck. When Gideon and Benjamin finally joined the rest of the family, Faith was still standing at the stove, assessing what was now her own small family. She felt a moment of joy as though being washed over with a wave of happiness. In all of her life, she never would have thought this was possible: moving into the empty place that Rebecca, the nurturing and loving wife and mother, had so unexpectedly vacated. Not as the former Faith, the girl who wanted to learn as much as she could, who wanted to teach children in school, and who never had given much thought of having her own family.

Despite all of that, she felt true bliss and, when Manuel looked up, folding the paper and setting it on the floor beneath his chair, she smiled at him. "Are you ready then?" she asked as she began to carry the plates of food over to the table.

"Danke, Faith," he said softly as she set the food before him. "It looks right gut." He glanced around the table. "Shall we pray?" He didn't wait for an answer as he lowered his head. The children did the same and Faith followed suit, shutting her eyes and saying a brief, silent prayer over the food.

Please let me keep this family together and bless them with my love, she prayed. *Please help me be a good mamm to these kinner and a strong partner for Manuel.*

When Manuel cleared his throat and looked up, the time for prayer was over and the food was passed around the table.

"Seems like we have ourselves a busy weekend, ain't so?" he said, his voice sounding strained and forced. Faith sensed it immediately. For the first time, they were sitting around the kitchen table as a family. Immediately, she knew that they were all battling with memories, memories of other breakfast meals shared with their mamm...their real mamm. Despite Faith having shared meals with the children before, it hadn't been too often that Manuel had joined them, at least not for a family breakfast.

Faith tried to sound normal, but she felt nervous inside. "What is planned for the weekend, Manuel?"

He glanced at her and then quickly looked at each of his children. "Visiting on Saturday after chores. Have to visit family, Faith. Pay our respects to them. Then Sunday is church at the Zook's." He quickly clarified by adding "Aaron Zooks."

Visiting? Faith had heard about this custom, remembering it from when Rebecca was married. After the wedding, the couple was supposed to visit family on the weekends. She hadn't given much thought to it, hadn't considered that it would apply to a second wife. But then again, it made sense. The family wanted to properly welcome her as one of their own. It was the Amish version of a honeymoon.

"I see," she responded softly.

She noticed that he peeked at her before bending his head back down to his breakfast. "They'll be wanting to get to know you, Faith," he said gently. "We all do."

We all do. His words resonated in her head. Was that what he thought? That he had married her but didn't know her? She realized that, despite the amount of time that she had been at his farm, helping with the children, she didn't know Manuel at all. It dawned on her that if her decision to step into the world of the Amish and to take over the raising of the children had seem brash, so was his to accept her into his home.

You help Manny had been Rebecca's last words. She had wanted this. She had directed Faith to step into this role, to raise her best friend's children, and to help her best-friend's husband. It had been her dying wish. A wish that was now irreversible.

"Well," Faith finally said, setting her fork down on her plate and staring directly at Manuel. "I reckon today is as good as any to start that process, yes?"

He seemed surprised by how direct she spoke to him. Yet, it was clear that the kinner didn't understand the underlying meaning.

By the time that Faith had packed the lunch pails for the children and walked them outside, it was almost eight o'clock. She stood on the porch, watching as the five of them traipsed down the driveway toward the road, Benjamin doing his best to keep up with the others. At one point, Sadie turned around, shielding her eyes from the morning sun to see if Faith was still watching. When she saw that Faith still stood on the porch, Sadie waved her hand enthusiastically over her head.

Faith laughed and waved back, leaning against the pole on the porch.

"They love you."

She glanced over her shoulder, surprised to see Manuel standing behind her, his frame filling the open kitchen door. He stared at her, his eyes narrowed just a touch as if he was studying her again. He wore a sky blue shirt covered by his black work vest. His brown hair covered his ears in the typical Amish fashion. But there was something about him, something that made her heart skip a beat as he stood there, watching her.

"I love them, too," she finally whispered. And she meant it.

"I wonder..." he said but stopped midsentence. For a moment, he kept staring at her, his eyes squinting, just a touch, as the sun was behind her. Then, without another word, he took a step forward and reached for Faith's hand. His skin was warm and the gesture startled her. She wasn't certain how to react but didn't have time to think. He held it in his own and pulled her toward him, his eyes pausing to glance over her head to make certain the children were out of sight. Then, he looked down into her face and, with his free hand, slowly traced his finger along her cheek. "Mayhaps one day you will love me, too?"

The way he was looking at her and the way that he held her against his body made her catch her breath. She felt as if he could see into her soul, glimpsing all of her thoughts and understanding everything that she was feeling. The gentle way that his finger brushed against her skin sent shivers up her spine and she had to look away, uncertain of how to respond. Oh, there were some things that she was starting to love about him, mostly things that revolved around the children. She just wished that she knew him in a way that would break down the barrier to true love, the type of spiritual love between husband and wife, between friends and partners in everything.

"Ja," he said softly. "One day." And with that, he leaned down and gently, oh so very gently, pressed his lips against hers, the gesture startling her so much that she didn't know how to react. When he pulled back, his eyes still staring into hers, she saw the slightest hint of a smile on his lips. "But not today," he whispered, his breath just barely caressing her face, and then backed away.

She was breathless from the kiss and could only watch as he reached inside the door for his straw hat, smiling to himself as he walked past her on his way to the barn. She leaned against the wall of the house and stared after him, noticing a more confident swagger to his walk. He had left her stunned, completely speechless, and more than a little shocked with what had been their first kiss, something she hadn't expected and, frankly, found her yearning for more. Something had sparked within her, an attraction that she hadn't even known existed; or perhaps an attraction that simply had been buried very deep in her consciousness, repressed because of the fact that he was Amish and that she was not. Until now, she thought.

You have to save her, Manuel! Save her!

Rebecca's words rang in Faith's ears as if Rebecca were standing right beside her. Immediately, the image of him hovering over her, his hand under her neck and his face so close to hers suddenly flashed before her eyes, rekindled by his kiss. The memory of how, way back when, he had leaned down to press his lips against her cold, practically lifeless ones as she had laid near-death on the embankment, drenched in her dress with Rebecca standing nearby, her hands clasped together and tears streaming down her face.

And then, all at once, she realized that the spark was nothing new at all. It had been there all along. But even more startling was the fact that she understood that she was not the first to know it. From the look in his eyes and the way he had kissed her, she realized that he had known that all along as well.

She stood there, stunned and moved. Her first kiss from her husband had taken away her breath and left her weak in the knees but the first time his lips had touched hers, so many, many years ago, Manuel had given her the kiss of life. And Faith understood at this moment that there must have been a higher purpose in what had transpired on that day than just to spare her own life: His divine will.

Manuel disappeared into the barn and she took the time to catch her breath. She felt a warmth flow throughout her veins as she replayed those few seconds in her memory. Manuel had kissed her. Manuel had reached for her and held her, his lips pressed against hers as a true husband should kiss a wife. She lifted her hands to touch her mouth, surprised to realize that she was trembling. She hadn't expected such affection, not from Manuel, not now...perhaps not ever. Her eyes fluttered back toward the barn, the direction in which he had disappeared.

Her husband.

From inside, she heard the baby cry, fussing from the high chair where she had been left. The noise brought Faith back to the present and, pushing the memory of that kiss, that surprisingly wonderful kiss, out of her mind, Faith hurried back inside, gushing as she collected Ruthie in her arms, smothering the baby with kisses to make up for having left her alone during those past few minutes.

For the rest of the morning, Faith found herself constantly pausing and staring out the window, hoping to catch a glimpse of Manuel. When she realized what she was doing, she would lower her head and blush, forcing herself to refocus on the task at hand, whether it was sorting the laundry, dusting the wooden furniture, or washing the dishes. Yet, she couldn't get that feeling of butterflies out of her stomach whenever she thought about that kiss. It had been so unexpected, so gentle, so passionate. More than anything, she wondered what he had meant. *Not today*, he had said.

Not today *what*?

She had fed the baby and set her down for a nap when she heard the door open. Glancing at the clock, she saw that it was almost one o'clock, well past the dinner hour. She leaned back and peeked toward the door, waiting to see if Manuel was coming into the kitchen. She could hear him moving about in the washroom, setting something heavy down on the floor and pushing aside what sounded like wood. Curious, she wiped her hands on her apron and walked toward the door into the outer room.

He was kneeling before the brick cook stove, putting wood in the opening. He didn't realize that she was watching him as he began to crumple up old newspaper and shove it under the wood. He reached into his pocket as if looking for something that he couldn't find.

"A match?" she asked softly.

He looked over his shoulder at her, startled to see her there but his expression immediately softened. "Ja," he said. "Would you mind? There's a strike pad..." He started to point but she was already moving toward the metal box on the wall where the matches were kept. She lit it and carried it carefully over to him. "Danke," he said as he took the match, his fingers brushing against hers during the pass off.

She stood back and watched as he lit the fire, still kneeling before the cook stove. When the paper caught fire, he blew gently on it, pleased with the way the kindling began to spark and flame. Tossing the match into the opening, he leaned his hand on the edge of the cook stove and stood up, towering over her. "For you," he said, his eyes twinkling as if he had a big secret that he was keeping from her.

"For me?"

He nodded and pointed toward a tall bucket on the counter. "Ja, for you, Faith. Today you will learn how to make cheese."

For a second, she stared at him, wondering whether or not he was teasing her again. Cheese? Not even her own mother had ever made cheese."Whatever for?"

He laughed at her and she realized that it was one of the first times in a long time that she had heard him genuinely laugh. There was something so relaxed about him, a transformation that had occurred in just one day. She found herself drawn toward him, this new Manuel, hoping that he would continue to stay in the house so she could be near him. "Why, I can think of several things to do with cheese...I happen to like some well-made Colby cheese," he said. "But with all this milk, it sure is nice to sell it, too."

Faith stared at the cook stove then over at the container

of milk. "Why..." she started before looking back at him, stunned at his expectation that she would know how to make cheese, "I would have no idea how to do that!"

She saw him purse his lips as if suppressing a smile and he raised one eyebrow, tilting his head as he looked at her. "Mayhaps I could show you, then?"

Oh. She caught her breath and felt her pulse quicken. At that very moment, she realized that she would like nothing more than for Manuel to spend that time with her, to show her how to do something, to be near her for some alone time without children nearby. Nodding her head, she took a step backward, allowing him to walk past her toward the pantry that was located off the side of the washroom. He pushed a few things aside on the shelves before he found what he was looking for: a large, metal pot.

He gave her a quick smile as he set the pot on the counter by the sink. "I reckon everything would be here," he said, leaving the rest of what he meant unspoken. Certainly no one had made cheese in the house since Rebecca had passed away. The realization that they were touching something that had last been used by Rebecca gave them both reason to pause, but only for a moment.

Faith wanted to ask the question, to learn what he was thinking. But she had quickly remembered that the Amish didn't speak too often of those that had passed on to walk with Jesus. Questions were often met with silence so she knew better than speak what was on her mind. Instead, she placed her hand on the rim of the large pot, letting her fingers brush against his once again. When he looked at her, she smiled and met his gaze. "How do we get started, Manuel?"

His thoughts broken, he nodded his head and turned his

attention back to the pot. "Right, we need to get started." He took a deep breath and began to explain to her how the process worked. The milk needed to be heated to 84 degrees. He lifted a long thermometer from inside the pan and showed her how it clipped onto the side. "It shouldn't get much hotter than that, Faith," he said. "Certainly not boil. Then you put in the culture and the rennet." He glanced into the pot and, not finding what he was looking for, hurried back into the pantry and moved aside several jars. "Here it is," he announced as he walked back to the counter, carrying a plastic bag with small, white packages in it.

"What's that?"

He showed her the different packages that were labeled. "This is the culture. You will use two of these for one large pot of milk. And these," he said as he pulled out a white box with red writing on it. "These are the rennet tablets. I recommend diluting them in warm milk before you put them into the pot. Again, use two."

"Two," she repeated softly, trying to commit his instructions to memory.

"Keep it at 86 degrees for about an hour or so, I reckon. Whatever you do, do not stir it, ja? Eventually, you'll see the curds form. When that happens, you come get me and I'll show you what to do next." He leaned his hip against the counter and watched her, his arms crossed lightly across his chest and a smile on his lips. "You think you can remember all that, then?"

"Well, I can try," she said. "Doesn't sound too hard for a former school teacher"

He laughed and reached out, lightly touching her chin in a teasing gesture. "We shall see about that." He was still chuckling as he reached for his hat and placed it on his head before walking back outside. She stared after him, smiling to herself at this new, relaxed Manuel. She couldn't quite understand what had changed since the night before. He had seemed so tense and distant during the wedding service and ceremony. Back at the house afterwards, he had all but avoided her. Yet, this morning he had woken up as though he was a new man.

And, indeed, she liked the new Manuel. There was a charm to him, a manner of carrying himself that was exactly as Lydia had said: kind and gentle. And, of course, there had been that surprising kiss earlier that morning on the porch, a kiss of hope and a promise for a future, a real future, as husband and wife.

For the next hour, she hovered near the wood burning cook stove, loving the smell of the fire that crackled beneath the heavy metal grate sitting on top of it. The room was warm and she didn't mind. She knew that it was cold outside. She had poured the milk into the large pot and set it upon the grate, watching the thermometer carefully as the liquid heated up. When it reached 84 degrees, she did as Manuel had instructed: removed some milk to dissolve the rennet tables before pouring that with the culture back into the liquid.

She stirred it gently and checked the thermometer again. 86 degrees. Frowning, she tried to think about how to get the liquid to cool back down. She couldn't stop the fire and, as she watched, the thermometer began to increase steadily: 87 degrees, 88 degrees.

She reached for two towels and, carefully, lifted the pot above the grate for a few seconds. It was heavy but she waited until the temperature decreased. Yet, when she put the pot back on the grate, the thermometer started to rapidly rise again. "Oh help," she muttered and looked around the room for something, anything, to give her an idea. She couldn't stand there indefinitely holding that heavy pot filled with five gallons of milk.

Her eyes caught on a set of bricks in the corner of the room. Immediately, an idea formed in her mind and she hurried over to get the bricks. Then she moved the pot off the grate, layered the bricks on top of it, and put the pot back onto the oven, only this time lifted above and resting on two layers of bricks. The temperature of the milk remained steady at 87 degrees. Good enough, she thought, pleased with her ingenuity. Yet, within minutes, the temperature began to rise again. For a moment, she contemplated seeking out Manuel to ask for his advice but she didn't want to bother him while he was working. If only she could call her mother, she thought, but, without a phone in the house, that was impossible.

Determined, Faith leaned down and poked at the wood that burned under the grate. She spread the smoldering logs apart and peeked at the thermometer to see if that helped. The temperature seemed to hold steady at 85 degrees so Faith covered the pot and returned to the kitchen to finish preparations for the evening meal. She was going to make a nice meal: fried chicken and mashed potatoes, a hearty meal for the children after a long day at school and a long walk home

It was almost three o'clock when the baby began to cry. She quickly washed the flour from her hands and hurried upstairs to retrieve Ruthie. The children would be home from school soon, just in time to help her with the baby and the evening chores. She knew that the two boys would join their father outside, cleaning stalls and feeding the cows while he began the evening milking.

She realized that she was looking forward to the return of the children. She'd be glad for the company.

"Baby's up then?"

She turned around, surprised to see Manuel walking into the kitchen. He set his hat on the counter and moved to the sink to wash his hands. Drying them on a towel, he approached Faith and reached out for Ruthie. The gesture surprised Faith for she had rarely seen him hold the baby, at least not when she had been around. Of course, she realized that she had rarely seen him at all during the day and she hadn't been there at night.

"You must be hungry," she said, watching as he held Ruthie in his arms, tickling her chin with his beard. "Shall I make you something?"

He lifted his eyes and, peering over Ruthie's head, he met her gaze. "That would be right gut," he said. "Perhaps just some buttered bread to hold me over until supper." He returned his attention to Ruthie but kept talking to Faith. "Was too wrapped up in my chores. Forgot about dinner today."

She hurried about the kitchen, getting the table set so that he could eat properly. Besides setting out some sliced bread, she made certain to include some fresh fruit, jam, and butter next to his plate so that he could pick and choose what he wanted to eat.

She sat next to him on the bench, holding Ruthie while he bent his head in silent prayer before he reached for the bread and began to butter it.

"Curds are looking good," he said. "Need a bit of time to cool though. I had to put some more wood on the fire."

She had forgotten about the cheese.

"Tomorrow," he began. "We'll be visiting family in the

afternoon." He took a bite of the bread. "Anna will watch the children while we go," he added when he had swallowed the food in his mouth. "We don't have to stay long and I need to get back in time for the evening chores. But we have to pay our respects to the family, let them congratulate us proper, ja?"

Inwardly, she dreaded that. It was bad enough that she felt awkward and uncomfortable at the fellowship meal after church on Sundays, but to have to visit with his family, engage in conversation? She was still feeling her way through the routine of her new lifestyle. Lydia had, indeed, been a great help. But Faith felt shy around the others, too concerned about what they might think of her and her decision to join the Amish church and marry Manuel.

But she said nothing of this. She knew that Manuel was the head of the household and she wasn't meant to argue with him. She had learned that wives were to respect the husband and his guidance for the family. She had committed to do just that when she stood before the congregation and married him.

When Manuel had finished eating, he glanced at the clock and pushed his plate back. "Mayhaps we should see about those curds, ja? Kinner will be home soon and Anna can help with the pressing." He stood up and motioned for Faith to come with him.

She carried Ruthie with her and stood beside Manuel as he took the cover from the pot. She peered inside, noticing that there was both a liquid and a solid inside of it. "Why, look at that!" she exclaimed.

He laughed at her enthusiasm. "The liquid is the whey. We cut the curds and cook for another 15 minutes before we pour off the whey." She watched as he took a long, thin blade and began to cut the curds in one direction before rotating the pot and doing the same thing in the other direction. He covered the pot once again and bent down to put in another log. "Needs to get to 102 degrees for about an hour."

She watched as he poked at the logs. Satisfied, he stood back up. "Now we wait," he said.

"We wait," she repeated, shifting Ruthie in her arms.

He studied her face for a minute. He looked serious as he stared at her, his eyes slightly narrowed, just enough so that they looked crescent shaped. She rubbed Ruthie's back, feeling the baby pulling at the strings of her prayer kapp. Smiling, she reached up and loosened Ruthie's grip before the baby could pull the kapp off her head. At the same moment, Manuel reached out and took the baby from her again. He leaned down to set his daughter on the floor, his body blocking Ruthie from being able to get too close to the fire. Then, he took Faith's hand in his, caressing her skin with his thumb.

"Faith," he said, his eyes still studying hers. His voice was low and soft, something tender in it that made the color flood to her cheeks. He pulled her into his embrace, his one arm wrapped around her waist and the other holding her hand which he pressed against his heart.

"I...I..." She wasn't certain what she wanted to say. She wished she felt comfortable enough to tell him that she was nervous and frightened, yet excited at the same time. She wished she could tell him that she appreciated his patience with her but she wasn't ready yet. She wished she could tell him that, despite her apprehension, she was quickly realizing that she wanted to be ready to be a true wife. But none of those words came from her lips.

"We can wait," he whispered, as if reading her mind.

The door to the kitchen slammed open. Both Faith and

Manuel turned in the direction of the kitchen, listening as the children stomped into the room. They had used the other kitchen door, not the one by the washroom. For that, Faith was thankful. Otherwise, she realized, they would have interrupted that moment with Manuel even more than they just had by returning home in such a noisy fashion.

She took a deep breath and slowly withdrew her hand from Manuel's. She certainly didn't want the children to see her being in such an intimate embrace with their father. It simply wasn't proper.

"Ja, vell then," he said, his eyes darting away from Faith's as he took a step back and reached down to pick up Ruthie. Gently flipping the baby around so that her padded bottom rested in the crook of his arm, Manuel sighed and glanced toward the kitchen. "Must be time for afternoon chores, I reckon."

"Must be," she said softly, her heart pounding inside of her chest. She wondered what he had been about to say. The look in his eyes had spoken of something deep and thoughtful. She wished that she had shared a few more minutes alone with as she knew that such time wouldn't come again until the following Monday when the kinner would return to school. Of course, there would be time alone later that evening and, at the thought, she felt a mixture of nervousness and excitement.

We can wait.

She knew, however, that he had not been referring to the curds. He had, indeed, been referring to their relationship. There was something exciting about his approach to their marriage. He wasn't rushing her and for that, she was grateful. Yet, she found that she was beginning to long for more time alone with Manuel. Regardless of her true feelings for him, she knew that he was her husband for the rest of her life. Having seen a new side of him, a side that she realized he had held back from her until they were officially wed, she wanted to know more about him. To spend private time with him.

He held Ruthie while leaning over, his lips just beside her ear as he whispered, "We'll continue this later, ja?" Without waiting for an answer, he carried Ruthie into the kitchen and greeted the other children.

"Oh Faith!" Anna sang as she hurried into the washroom. "I mean Mamm," she quickly corrected, laughing at herself. "You're making cheese! How wunderbaar!" She lifted the lid of the pot and raised an eyebrow. "Why, that looks right perfect!" Clearly, she was impressed. "Did you ever make it with my mamm?"

The question surprised Faith. "Why no, I didn't," she responded. "But your daed helped me, to be truthful."

"My daed?" She laughed at the thought. "I never saw him making cheese before!"

Anna quickly began to take charge, helping Faith drain the whey when it was ready, and then, after washing her hands, showing her how to crumble the curds and salt them. Afterwards, Anna disappeared into the pantry and came back with two molds, showing Faith how to line the molds with cheese cloth and place the curds inside.

"Now we just need the presses and that's it until later tonight," Anna said proudly. "I can't wait. Haven't had fresh cheese in a while."

"Well," Faith said, uncertain that those soft white curds would amount to much. "I have to trust you on that one."

When the door opened, Manuel walked in with Gideon trailing behind him. Both were carrying large wooden apparatuses. Each was made of three pieces of wood: a base, a back, and a long, wooden lever that was resting on the base, forming a triangle. There were V-shaped notches in the lever. They were stained a dark brown, although one looked older than the other, with scratches and chips all over the wood. Manuel set his on the counter by the sink and reached for Gideon's to do the same.

"What in the world is that?" Faith exclaimed.

Manuel tried to hide his smile as Anna looked at her, not really surprised that Faith didn't know what she was looking at. "Those are cheese presses. Haven't you seen them before?"

Truth be told, Faith had no idea what a cheese press was or what it was for.

Anna clicked her tongue and rolled her eyes as she quickly showed Faith how to place the plastic mold with the cheese curds on the base. "Gideon," she said, pointing toward the pantry. "Go get those jugs of water right quick." Turning back to Faith, Anna explained. "We hang the jugs on this here lever and place a wedge in the notches so that it puts pressure on the mold. That pushes the excess water out of the curds and, eventually, they harden into a nice round of cheese." As if on cue, Gideon returned with the two jugs of water and handed them to Anna. She lifted them up and looped the string from the handle to the lever.

"Why, isn't that clever!" Faith said, amazed at the ingenuity.

Manuel laughed, not able to contain himself anymore. "Clever today, ja," he said. "But burdensome when you are making cheese *every* day."

Every day? She looked at him, stunned by this proclamation. Was she truly supposed to do this every day? He winked at her and placed his hand on Gideon's shoulder, guiding his son toward the door of the washroom. They were still chuckling as they left the house, heading toward the barn.

Faith turned back to Anna. "Did your daed say *every day*?"

"Ja," she nodded before quickly adding, "But not on Sunday, of course."

"Every day?" She was still hung up on the concept of having to do that every day.

Even Anna had to laugh. "It's not that much work and we sell the excess to neighbors or the Englische. They pay top dollar for home-made Amish cheese."

"They do, do they?"

"Oh ja!" Anna wiped her hands on her black apron. "We used to make it every day, too," she said. "Mamm would vacuum seal it and store it in the freezer, the one Daed has in the garage. Then, come spring, we'd sell it from Lydia's house. She always has a busy stand because of the road she's on."

"I see." Faith was impressed with Anna's business acumen, despite only being twelve years old.

She loved visiting the Yoder house. The kitchen was the heart of the home and it was always filled with wonderful smells and special treats. Rebecca's mamm usually had fresh baked bread on wire cooling racks near the window and plastic Tupperware filled to the rim with the world's best sugar cookies. Without fail, Faith would follow Rebecca into the kitchen and a sugar cookie would find its way into her hand.

"Just one," Rebecca's mamm would say. "Can't have you spoiling your supper now."

One day, when Faith was getting ready to leave for home, Rebecca's mamm said something in Pennsylvania Dutch to her daughter. Immediately, Rebecca scurried to the propane-powered refrigerator and pulled out a large chunk of something, sealed in yellow wax. She grinned as she handed it to Faith. "I made this," Rebecca said.

"What is it?" Faith took it and turned it over in her hands. "Wax?"

Rebecca laughed and her mamm had to turn away to hide the twisting of her mouth at Faith's comment. "No, you goose! It's cheese!"

"Cheese?" Faith had never thought much about making cheese. In her household, cheese was bought at the store, not made in the kitchen. "Wow, Rebecca, I'm impressed."

"Mamm says you should take that home for your folks." There was an element of pride in her voice. "It's gut to share, ja?"

"Why would you make cheese?" Faith asked innocently. She was still lingering on the vision in her head of her friend not only knowing how to make cheese but in being so happy to do so. "Is it hard?"

"Nee," Rebecca said. "Mayhaps I'll show you one day. We can make it together." She glanced over her shoulder at her mamm. "Right mamm?"

Faith carried her yellow wax block of cheese in her hand the entire way home, determined to ask her mother if Mennonites knew how to make cheese at home. By the time she arrived home and handed her mother the cheese, it was time for evening chores. Faith forgot to ask her mother about Mennonites and cheese making. And, before long, both Rebecca and Faith forgot to spend a day in the kitchen, huddled over a large steel pot filled with milk, in order to learn the special process of how *to make cheese.*

Supper was over and the kitchen had been cleaned. With the three girls helping her, Faith found it was very easy to keep everything tidy. They were willing to help, if properly directed. With the sun setting earlier, the sky was dark and Manuel lit the propane lantern. As the flame from the match touched the duct at the top of the lantern, a gentle hiss escaped and a bright glow of light brightened the room. Faith had learned long ago to never look at the flame. To do so meant seeing flashes of light for at least five minutes.

She watched as Manuel picked up a newspaper, The Budget, and sat down in his reading chair to peruse the news of the Amish communities around the country.

Faith wasn't certain about what to do. At home, she would have read a book or sat at the kitchen table talking with her mother. With the kitchen back in order, Faith had nothing else to do for the evening. She chewed on her lower lip, looking around the kitchen, willing something...anything...to jump at her that needed attention. There was just nothing else to do.

Lingering near the hutch behind the kitchen table, Faith sighed and reached for the Ausbund, the version that Manuel had given to her. She pulled the two volumes from the shelf and walked over to the sofa. She chose the first volume and flipped it open to where she had left a crocheted bookmark, one that Lydia had taught her how to make during her time living at that farm. Lydia had been most resourceful, teaching Faith many different things during the evenings. Faith made a mental note to send her a card of appreciation with a crocheted dishcloth of her own making.

"What are you reading, then?"

She looked up, startled at his attention. "Hmm?"

He gestured with his head to the book in her hand. "You are reading the Ausbund, ja? Which verse, Faith?"

Her heart fluttered as she saw him fold the paper and set it neatly on the table next to his chair. He stood up and took two steps to cross the space between them. "Oh, I...well, I thought I would start with this verse..." She pointed to the page. "I like the words."

He smiled as his eyes glanced at the left hand side of the page, the page printed in High German. "Ja," he said, obviously pleased with her selection. "I like that one, too."

She didn't know what to say in response.

"Shall I teach you the German words, then?"

Oh, she thought. When he had given her the books so many weeks ago, he had mentioned that he would do that, teach her the German pronunciation for the different verses in the Ausbund. Shyly, she nodded her head. "That would be nice, Manuel."

The kinner sat on the chair that Manuel had abandoned, the five of them crowding around each other and hanging off the arms. Benjamin sat on Anna's lap, laughing as Manuel patiently tried to teach Faith the proper way to speak High German. "This looks like an F but it's pronounced with an *essh* sound," he explained.

"That seems silly," she said. "Why don't they just use an S then?"

Sadie and Benjamin giggled and even Mary had to hide her smile. Indeed, it was a show for the children and, with a twinkle in his eye, Manuel played along. "Mayhaps you are right! We shall ask the bishop to change so many years of tradition and rewrite the Ausbund with an S for the F!" At this, even Anna burst out laughing, covering her mouth with her hand.

The lesson continued, Manuel leaning over Faith's shoulder, his arm pointing to the words as he said them, waiting patiently for Faith to repeat them. When she struggled with the word, he said it again, slowly enunciating each syllable. They went through a line at a time, making it through the first two verses in thirty minutes. When they finished, Manuel smiled his approval. "Dat ist gut, my fraa," he said, teasingly calling her the Pennsylvania Dutch word for "wife", the word rolling off his tongue easily for the first time. "Soon you will be singing in church with the rest of us, ja?"

"Oh I'm not so sure about that," she countered but then quickly added, "Unless you have a lot of patience teaching me."

He tilted his head and met her gaze, giving a single nod of his head. "I have patience, ja," he replied, his voice low and soft.

Too aware that the children were watching and feeling too much heat from Manuel's gaze, Faith gently reached for the books, taking them back from Manuel. "I reckon that's enough for one night, yes?" She stood up and replaced the books on the shelf before glancing at the clock. "And I suspect it should be time for bed soon."

Benjamin and Sadie groaned but only momentarily for both Anna and Manuel shot them a look, a look that told them to be quiet and not sass their new mamm. Within twenty minutes, the kinner had retreated upstairs and, after checking on Ruthie, Faith found herself, once again, alone with Manuel. She walked to the kitchen sink and fussed with the faucet, glancing once over her shoulder at him as he sat back in his chair with The Budget.

"Would you like some coffee or something?" she asked, trying to break the ice.

He looked up and peered at her. "Nee, but danke," he answered before taking a deep breath and folding the paper. "Reckon I should follow your advice, Faith. We do have a long day tomorrow with visiting family and all." Once again, he stood up and waited by the lantern, pausing for just a moment before reaching as if to turn it off. "You get started to the room, then," he said before quickly adding. "I'll join you shortly."

She nodded and walked across the floor, her heart fluttering as she did. She felt the same apprehension as the previous evening when Manuel had announced that it was time to retire. Would he expect something from her tonight? Was she ready for such intimacy? Her heart pounded inside of her chest as she changed from her clothing, carefully putting them on the hanger before hanging them on the pegs that hung from the wall. It only took her a few minutes to change into her nightgown, a simple white gown of soft cotton. She had set her prayer kapp on the dresser and was brushing her hair when he entered.

The light from the lantern cast a soft, orange glow throughout the room. Shadows danced upon the walls. Nervously, she turned to face him, realizing that he was going to undress in front of her. She glanced at the floor as she averted her eyes, too aware that she had never seen a man without clothing. The previous evening, he had retired first and, when she had entered the room, he had already been in bed, his back to her, giving her much needed privacy.

"I...I can leave the room," she whispered demurely.

"Nee," he replied, a catch in his voice. "It's alright. You

are my wife, ja?"

As if she needed a reminder. It was what she had been thinking about all day, butterflies in her stomach at the realization. Instead, Faith nodded and started to walk to her side of the bed. As she passed him, she felt his hand on her arm, holding her back. Another flutter in her chest and she lifted her eyes to look into his face.

To her surprise, he reached out and touched her cheek, his fingers just lightly brushing against her skin before traveling to her loose hair. It was long and hung over her shoulders, almost straight save from the wave that had occurred from having it wrapped in a bun all day. He didn't speak, just stared at her as he quietly played with her hair, letting it slip through his fingers. His eyes moved, just momentarily, as he glanced at her nightgown and she thought she saw his cheeks redden. She was certain that hers did, too.

"It was a gut day, ja?" he whispered.

She nodded.

"You are happy enough?"

Happy enough? She wondered what he meant. "I am happy, yes," she replied.

He leaned down and gently pressed his lips against hers. "That is enough for tonight, then, ja?" And with that, he released her and walked toward his side of the bed, removing his suspenders before he took off his shirt and hung it on the wall. She turned her back, wondering at his words, why he had said that, but understanding, at the same time, that he was expecting nothing from her once again. This time, there was a mixture of confusion with her wave of relief.

Chapter Twelve

She sat in the living room on the sofa next to Manuel. The room was quiet except for the creaking of the rocking chair and the ticking of the clock on the wall. When they had entered the house, Faith had immediately been taken aback by how sparse everything was. The kitchen was pristine, nary an object on the counter and the table covered in a very simple green and white checkered tablecloth. The white linoleum floor, so typical in the Amish homes, reflected the light from the propane lantern. There were no curtains on the windows, no magnets on the refrigerator. It was sparse and plain, more so than Faith had ever seen at any other Amish house.

It was the third family that they had visited during the late afternoon hours. Just as she had at the other houses, Faith felt awkward, her hands clasped on her lap and her hip just lightly touching Manuel's. His aunt and uncle stared at them from their respective chairs, the aunt rocking back and forth on an old wooden rocker.

"You getting on well then, ja?" the uncle finally said stiffly as he stared at Faith with dark eyes. His long, grey beard touched the second button of his white shirt. "Farm work not too much for you?"

Faith cleared her throat, wishing that Manuel would speak up. When he didn't, she finally responded with a simple response. "My father was a farmer so I'm used to rising early and greeting the sun." She tried to sound cheerful and upbeat when she responded but wasn't certain if that was the right thing to do. Most Amish women tended to be more subdued and quiet. Fidgeting beside Manuel, she wished that he would guide her in how to interact with his family members.

"I see," the uncle said. "What about your other bruders and schwesters?"

Faith hesitated, knowing that her response would sound awkward to an Amish man, a man used to large families with upwards of ten children on average. "I'm an only child."

The aunt caught her breath and stopped rocking her chair. Leaning forward, she stared hard at Faith. "And your parents are Mennonite?" She looked at her husband. "A Mennonite farmer with only one child?" She shook her head, the too familiar *tsk-tsk* escaping her lips.

Faith flushed at the reprimand, feeling as if she had to defend her parents' choice. "Yes, I was raised Mennonite. But my mother had a condition," she said softly. "The doctors told her to not have more children for fear of dying. It was a miracle that she had me, I'm told."

From the corner of her eye, she noticed Manuel stiffen at her words and felt the heat of his eyes on her neck. She glanced at him, wondering why he was staring at her. He had known that she was an only child. Certainly Rebecca had told him that and explained that it was due to her mother's medical condition. But, as this thought went through Faith's mind, she immediately realized that Manuel must have been thinking of Rebecca. Inwardly, Faith scolded herself for having said too much without thinking ahead.

Indeed, the room fell silent at her comment. The silence felt awkward to Faith. She prayed that the visit would end quickly for she wanted nothing more than to retreat back to the farm, to end this awful day of sitting in living rooms, meeting people that she barely knew or had only just met at the wedding two days prior. Each visit had been uncomfortable for Faith. She could feel Manuel's family assessing her, trying to size up this new member of their family. Some of them had known her as Rebecca's friend from childhood. All of them seemed puzzled by her decision to become a baptized member of the Amish church.

"I have something for you, Faith," the aunt finally said, standing up and excusing herself as she bustled out of the room. Faith wasn't certain whether she should follow the woman and decided to stay seated next to Manuel, unless he directed her otherwise.

He didn't.

When the aunt returned, she was carrying a large box with white tissue sticking out of the open top. With great pride, she handed the box to Faith and smiled. "This was my mother's, Manuel's grandmother. I have no use for it now and all of my kinner are married. I hope you can put it to good use."

Faith smiled and lifted the tissue paper from the box. Inside was a large glass bowl, etched along the sides in a pretty floral design. "It's lovely," she said. "Danke." The word felt strange sliding off of her lips but the reaction from Manuel's aunt and uncle showed their delight in her attempt to speak Pennsylvania Dutch.

"Oh, you are learning our language!" the aunt said, smiling at Faith. "That's gut!"

Despite their pleasure, Faith felt awkward sitting there, the box on her lap. Manuel shared news about the kinner with his aunt and uncle before inquiring about his cousins' children. Faith sat there in silence, listening to the questions and not caring about the answers. She just wanted to return home.

When the Petersheim's finally left the house, Manuel

carrying the box as he led Faith toward the horse and buggy, Faith felt the urge to cry. It had been building up inside of her, a pressure in her chest and a lump in her throat. Her eyes began to sting as she fought the urge, not wanting to shame herself in front of Manuel. But the horrible realization continued to bother her: she was a stranger in this new world and she felt very out of place. Nothing was the same and yet she knew that, in reality, she was the one that was different. She was the outsider that had been, reluctantly, brought into the fold and now was expected to adapt.

"You all right?" he asked as he sat next to her in the buggy's front seat.

She wanted to nod her head, wanted to tell him that she was fine, but she couldn't. Words would not form on her lips. Instead, she burst into tears and covered her face with her hands, humiliated that she hadn't been able to contain her emotions and was crying before Manuel.

"Faith?" His voice was soft and tender, full of concern for her tears.

Choking back the sob, Faith waved her hand at Manuel, wishing she could speak. But the tears simply continued to flow down her cheeks and she couldn't say a word for fear of sobbing aloud.

Next to her, Manuel shifted his body so that he was facing her, the reins held in one hand as he reached up and brushed a stray hair from her forehead. "What is it, Faith? What's wrong?" In the dim light from the setting sun, she could see the worried look on his face and she knew that she had to respond.

"It's too much," she managed to say, trying to hide her face, still embarrassed about her outburst. "I don't fit in. I'll never fit in."

Softly, he chuckled under his breath and put his arm around her shoulders. He pulled her toward his chest, the intimacy of being in his arms startling her and causing her tears to stop flowing. Holding her, Manuel paused to gently kiss the top of her head, just where the prayer kapp was held to her hair with a straight pin. "Oh Faith," he murmured. "You are fitting in. In more ways than you can imagine."

"No," she said, shaking her head against his shoulder. "That's not true. Not true at all."

He pulled back and stared down into her tear stricken face. "How can you say that? You are doing a fabulous job with the kinner, with the house..."

"But not with you!" she interrupted, her voice a mere whisper.

"Me?" He seemed genuinely startled by her admission. "I should be the least of your worries."

Again, she shook her head. "Nee," she said. "You are the most of my worries."

He was silent for a moment, his eyes studying her in the slight glow from the battery-powered dashboard. "Me?"

She lifted her hand to her head, putting her fingers over her eyes as she pushed back the pain of the emotions she was feeling. She didn't know how to explain it to him. Despite the amount of time that had passed, she felt as if everything had happened so quickly and she hadn't been prepared. Yet, in reality, she knew it had only been two days since their wedding. How could she expect to adapt so quickly? She had a lifetime ahead of her to adjust to her new life.

"Why me, Faith?" he asked.

"Oh, I don't know," she said, exasperated. "I guess...well,

I guess I just feel like life has moved on for everyone, just continued. But for me, it's all so overwhelming and different. Everything seems new and strange."

"What does that have to do with me?"

She dropped her hand and stared at him. "It has everything to do with you, Manuel. I want to feel comfortable with you, to know you and be your friend. But I feel like there is this barrier between us, an invisible shield that I can't quite understand." She paused. "How can I be a wife, a *true* wife, if there is a barrier?"

He reached out and wiped away her tears, a tender smile on his face. "Calm down, Faith," he murmured, compassion in his voice. "It will all be just fine. You need to give it more time. It will happen."

She wanted to believe him. "It will?"

"Ja, it will," he said softly. "Sooner than you'd imagine, no doubt. Indeed, I think we are well on the way to being friends, very good friends, and getting to know each other better."

She sniffled and reached her hand up to touch his. The gesture startled him and he tilted his head. She pressed her cheek against his hand and stared at him. "We are?"

He nodded. "Ja, we are."

She hesitated, just long enough to bite the corner of her lip as she held his gaze. Her courage grew within her and she clutched at his hand. "Then please, Manuel, please do me a favor."

That smile. Soft and tender. It warmed her heart when she saw it cross his lips. "Anything, Faith. Anything if it makes you feel better."

She shut her eyes and sighed. Yes, she thought. That was

exactly what she needed to hear. "Kiss me, Manuel. Please." She opened her eyes and looked at him. "Kiss me like you did yesterday on the porch."

Her request startled him. She could see that from his reaction. Yet, she saw him lean forward, slowly, and, with his hand on the back of her neck, he pulled her close to him. His lips found hers and, with a softness that she only remembered from her memory of the day before, he kissed her. Gentle, timid, and patient. She shut her eyes, feeling herself press against him, her hand touching his shoulder under his jacket, the fabric of his shirt soft against her hand and his muscles warm under her fingertips.

When he pulled away from her, he rested his forehead against hers and sighed. "Faith," he murmured, his eyes shut. "What are you doing to me?"

This time, it was Faith that was startled. "What *am I* doing to you?"

He sighed and shook his head slightly, lifting his hand to touch her cheek. "It's not time yet."

She felt a wave of frustration and wanted to tell him so. The reality of their marriage was dawning on her, the magnitude of their union creating her distress. She needed to forget the past and move forward, become his wife and feel like a wife. She needed to be more than a wife in name but in all aspects. But she didn't know how to tell him and she feared that doing so would be pushing it. Besides, deep down, she knew he was right. "I just need to know," she finally whispered.

"Know what?" His words were soft and tender, nothing accusing or judgmental. In the distance, a horse and buggy rattled down the road beside his uncle's farm. They listened to it, the noise musical as it approached. When the sound started to disappear again, the buggy moving further away, he caressed the side of her cheek. "Know what, Faith?" he repeated.

"That you care."

"Ah," he said, pulling back just a touch, a slight distance between them. "You need to know if I care, ja?" He chuckled under his breath, his finger still caressing her skin. "Do you really think that I would have agreed to marry you if I didn't?"

"But, the children..." she started to say, suddenly realizing how little thought she had put into the arrangement. It had been agreed upon, by both of them, under the guise of the children. Yet, in reality, she knew that there was something deeper between them, a seed that had sprouted roots many years ago but had lain dormant until just recently.

"The children, ja," he said gently. "But also you." He leaned forward again and gave her a soft, gentle but chaste kiss. "You showed me that my life must continue, Faith," he said. "Rebecca would have wanted that. The children want it. I want it, too. And I would prefer my life to continue with you by my side rather than anyone else."

Despite the abrupt end to the moment, she felt as if she had learned something, a marvelous something that made her warm inside. It was just what she needed to know, what she had wished she had known all along. Deep down, Manuel wanted to fall in love with her as much as she wanted to fall in love with him. Indeed, she thought as the buggy lurched forward and moved out of the driveway, the seed was beginning to grow, a new growth, sprouting through the dirt and reaching toward the sun. With enough nurturing, she thought, surely it would bloom into a beautiful flower that exuded love.

They rode home in silence, words now being unnecessary. The silence gave them both time to reflect on what had just happened. She felt him shift his weight, moving the reins back into one hand so that he could reach down with the other and hold hers. The timing of his tender gesture was perfect, the right touch at the right moment and her heart swelled, a wave of emotion washing over her. Indeed, if they had not courted before, he was giving her that time now so that they could become a real couple in time, a strong partnership with shared emotions, before either of them felt pressured for more. That realization caused her a moment of joy as she had never felt before and she said a silent prayer of thanksgiving to God for having guided her down this path.

The farm was dark when they pulled into the driveway. Manuel helped her off the buggy, pausing to squeeze her hand before motioning that she should go into the house while he untacked the horse. She reached into the back of the buggy and took the bowl that his aunt had given to them. "Send the boys out, ja?" he said quietly.

She nodded and hurried to the house.

From the porch window, she could see the bright glow emanating from the propane light in the kitchen. She was always amazed at how brilliant those lights glowed and had learned long ago to never look directly at one. Opening the door, she carefully balanced the bowl in her hand before she slipped inside. "Hello?" she called out, feeling strange as she entered the house. During her months of helping with the children, she had rarely been in the house at night. It felt odd entering it without Manuel beside her.

"Mamm?"

Sadie and Benjamin ran around the corner, laughing as

they tumbled into her. "Why, that's a lovely greeting!" she said, setting the bowl on the counter before she took off her black shawl to hang it on a peg. Then, bending down, she let both children hug her. "Certainly we weren't gone that long!"

"We've been waiting for you!" Sadie giggled, practically jumping up and down in delight.

"You have, have you?" she asked. "Whatever for?"

Mary blocked her from coming into the kitchen. "Wait for Daed," she said joyfully. "Wait for Daed before you come into the kitchen."

It didn't take long for Manuel to come inside to find out where the boys were. He had already unharnessed the horse. "*Wie gehts?*" he asked, taking off his hat. "I thought the boys were going to come help, ja?"

Faith raised her shoulders in a teasing shrug. "I've been held hostage here in the washroom until you came inside," she said lightly.

"Ah," he said, a twinkle coming to his eyes. "Vell, I am here now."

"Come see what we've done!" Sadie cried out happily, clapping her hands and laughing. Without waiting for an answer, Sadie grabbed Faith's hand and dragged her into the kitchen, Manuel following close behind.

"Oh help," Faith teased, delighted with the joyous welcome they had received upon their return.

As she stepped through the doorway of the washroom into the kitchen, she caught her breath and stood still. Anna and Mary stood by the counter, smiling broadly. Ruthie was in her high chair, waving a spoon in the air and gurgling happily. Even Gideon was nearby, a big grin on his face.

The table was set with a white tablecloth and fancy

plates at each seat. It was a special set of china that Faith had never seen before. Each of the glasses matched, unlike most nights when there was a mixture of glassware and plastic cups for water or milk. In the center of the table was a vase with pretty flowers in it which, upon closer inspection, Faith noticed were not real, a fact that touched her heart even more. "What on earth?" she said, taking in the scene before she looked at all of the children. "What is this?"

Sadie clapped her hands, barely able to contain herself. "We made you and Daed supper!"

Gideon stood by the sofa next to Benjamin, proudly puffing out his chest as he beamed at his daed. "And Ben and I...we already took care of the evening chores!" he said, a grin on his face.

Anna reached over and placed her hand on Sadie's shoulder. "We wanted to surprise you."

"Well," Faith started, fighting the all too familiar lump that grew in her throat. Only this time, it was for joy, not fear. "You sure did that." Indeed, the gesture touched her profoundly. The kindness and thoughtfulness of what the children had done, working together, while she and Manuel had been gone for the entire afternoon, spoke volumes about their character as well as how much they thought of others before themselves.

She glanced at Manuel and noticed that even he was moved. He cleared his throat and had to glance away for a moment. After the stress of the visits and their talk before the ride home, this was, indeed, a warm welcome from the part of the kinner.

They sat at the table and Manuel signaled for everyone to bow their heads in silent prayer. Faith shut her eyes and prayed to God, thanking Him for the many blessings of the day and asking for guidance in continuing to follow His word. Yet, even as she prayed these words in her mind, she felt a glow within her, one that let her know that He was pleased with her decisions. As the realization came, she felt lighter and calm, a peaceful sensation falling over her and she lifted her eyes, surprised to see Manuel watching her. Immediately, she blushed, wondering if he had seen her spiritual transformation during the prayer over a simple meal. Glancing away, she smiled at Anna who sat beside her, pausing just long enough to reach out her hand and touch the girl's arm.

"Danke, Anna," Faith said. "Your mother would be very proud of you."

Once again, after the meal, the three girls helped Faith while Manuel sat in his chair, this time holding Ruthie as she chewed on the ear of a stuffed bear that she held in her hands. The two boys were sent to take their Saturday bath so that, when the girls were finished, the rest of the family could wash in preparation for Sunday service.

"I'll take Ruthie," Faith said as she dried her hands on her apron before reaching for her. The baby cooed and giggled, holding out her arms for Faith to take her. "Someone needs a tubby, ja?"

Manuel looked up at her and tried to hide his smile. Benjamin and Gideon snickered amongst each other while Sadie made a funny face at her daed.

"What's so funny?" Faith asked, pretending to be offended.

He glanced at the children who had also heard Faith's use of the word "ja". It was clear that they all shared a secret chuckle but, rather than let her in, they merely shook their heads at Faith, proclaiming their innocence in any sort of teasing.

Faith raised an eyebrow, knowing full well what she had said but letting the father and his children share their private joke. Inside, her heart swelled with joy at the interaction between Manuel and the kinner. She was seeing a new side of him, one that was full of light and love. Just as Lydia had said, Manuel was full of surprises, tender and generous in nature. For the first time in months, Faith felt true happiness in the house.

By the time that all of the children were bathed and dressed for bed, it was almost nine o'clock. Tucking in the smaller children, Faith sat by their beds as she listened to their evening prayers. The older children prayed silently and didn't need her attention, beyond a pleasant "Good night and sleep tight!"

With darkness outside and the glow from the propane lamp filling the room, Faith felt the return of her nighttime jitters. She walked down the staircase, lingering briefly on the bottom step as she caught sight of Manuel standing by the window. He must have gotten up to retrieve a cup of water for the counter had been cleared before she went upstairs but now there was a blue plastic cup by the sink.

"Everything all right?" she asked, approaching him slowly so that she wouldn't startle him.

"Hmm?" He glanced over his shoulder and, as she neared, he reached out his hand. "Oh ja, ja," he said, waiting for her to place her hand in his. The gesture delighted her and she did as he expected. "I want you to know," he started, his head bowed down in a sign of humility. "I heard what you said earlier, Faith. What you said about needing to know that I care." He paused, pulling her closer, his eyes drifting just momentarily toward the stairs to ensure that they were, indeed, alone. Once he was reassured of their privacy, he stared down into her face, his eyes flickering back and forth as they traveled from her own eyes to her nose to her lips and then back to her eyes. "And I do."

"Manuel?"

Faith could tell that there was something on his mind, something that he wanted to say to her. But the words never passed his lips. There was a new energy between them and she felt her heart begin to flutter inside of her chest, a mixture of excitement and nervousness for what it might mean. Yet, rather than pursue the hint of intimacy that might close that gap between them, Manuel merely smiled a soft and tender smile. "We have a busy day tomorrow, Faith," he said. "I'll just go check on the barn, make certain the boys did everything proper and all. But we best be saying good night now. Have to get up extra early to get chores done before church." He leaned down and gently pressed his lips against her forehead, his hand lingering on her arm. "You go on and I'll join you a bit later."

This time, she was already asleep before he joined her. Almost an hour had passed since he had wandered outside, to where and for what, she didn't know. What she did know was that, two hours later, something disturbed her and she awoke. Manuel was next to her in the bed, his arm casually tossed over her waist, his soft breath caressing her neck as he slept. She shut her eyes, still half asleep, but content in the knowledge that he was there, with her, and comfortable enough to sleep with her in his arms.

Chapter Thirteen

After the church service, Faith held Ruthie in her arms as she stood among the other women. Most of them were conversing in Pennsylvania Dutch and Faith didn't understand what they were saying. Occasionally, when they realized that Faith was nearby, they would switch to English in order to include her in the conversation.

"So how you getting on then?"

Faith smiled at the older woman who had addressed her. "Just fine, danke," she replied. She shifted the baby in her arms and peered down at her. "The children have been wonderful."

"It's a right gut thing that you've done," the woman said, nodding her head. "I'm sure everyone is appreciative."

Scanning the room, Faith found Manuel. He was talking with some of the other men, listening intently to their conversation. Yet, he must have felt her eyes on him for, at the same moment, he looked up and met her gaze. For a brief second, no one else seemed to be in the room. She watched him, thinking back to the previous evening and how he had held her throughout the night, her back pressed against his chest. The color rose to her cheeks and she thought she saw him hiding a smile. Surely he had sensed what she was thinking about.

It was a half hour later when Manuel approached her. Gently, he touched her arm and leaned over to her ear. "You ready to go home?" She felt his warm breath on her bare neck and shivered before she nodded her head. "I'll harness the horse if you get the kinner then," he said, his hand still on her arm. Before he removed it, his thumb brushed gently against her skin. When he moved away, she felt a flutter in her chest and her eyes followed him.

Something had changed in him, something stoic and noble. She couldn't put her finger on it but she knew that Manuel was different. Gone was the mourning and sorrow. Instead, he had an aura of peace and contentment lingering over him, a happiness that filled him. The difference was more than apparent, especially if she reflected back to the previous spring.

They were quiet on the ride home, the four younger children in the back of the buggy and Anna situated at Faith's feet. Ruthie slept in Mary's arms, the gentle rocking of the buggy making everyone feel a bit sleepy. The sky was grey, overcast with low clouds and the air was crisp. It almost smelled as if it might snow.

"Might it snow?" she asked softly, her eyes on Manuel's face.

He glanced up at the sky through the buggy window. "Reckon it might. Sure feels like it."

"Good weather for sleeping," she replied then blushed at the unspoken insinuation. He glanced at her, one eyebrow raised. But he didn't respond.

At home, Gideon and Benjamin helped their father with the horse and buggy while Faith and the girls hurried inside. For the rest of the day, they would sit and play board games, spending time together, their first Sunday as a family. With the chill in the air, it was the perfect day for playing games.

"I wish we could crochet or quilt on Sunday," Anna said as she pulled out the Scrabble board and carried it to the table.

Manuel had just emerged from the washroom and hung his hat on the peg by the door. He slapped his arms against his chest. "You might be right, Faith. There sure is a bite to the air. Might just be our first snowfall!"

"Daed, why can't we quilt on Sundays?" Anna asked, kneeling on the bench and setting up the Scrabble board.

He walked into the room and headed for the sink to wash his hands. "Reckon the bishop feels Sundays should be spent resting and visiting, not working unless it's necessary."

"Quilting isn't work," she replied.

"Ja vell," he said, shaking the water from his hands. "Not our place to question the bishop, is it? Besides I am not so sure about your brothers and me crocheting or quilting," he added teasingly, to which Sadie and Mary simultaneously burst into laughter. Even Faith had to cover her mouth, hiding her amusement at Manuel's statement. "Dochder" he went on, "Scrabble may be more appropriate as something we can all do together as a family on a Sunday afternoon, don't you reckon?" He looked over at Faith, silent for a brief second before he tilted his head. "Mayhaps *you* might take to quilting and have a quilting bee this winter. You'll be wanting your own wedding quilt," he said softly. He paused. "Did I ever show you where Rebecca signed our quilt?"

The question took her by surprise. He rarely mentioned Rebecca and the reference to their wedding quilt startled her. Yet, she was even more surprised when he led her upstairs to the room where he had stayed when he was ill. She hadn't noticed that he had moved the wedding quilt from the downstairs bedroom to the upstairs room. When she realized that he had, she was conflicted. Part of her was struck by the symbolism of his action. Surely he had felt torn removing the quilt from the room downstairs. Yet, part of her was touched. He hadn't wanted to share the bed with his new bride sleeping under his first wife's quilt.

"Oh Manny," she whispered, her hand rising to her chest.

For a moment, he hesitated, taken aback by her two simple words. *Oh Manny*. His childhood nickname. The nickname that Rebecca despised and continually reprimanded Faith when she used it.

Manuel reached for her hand and held it for a moment. His fingers caressed her skin and he looked down into her face. "It's over here," he finally said, walking toward the bed and lifting the corner. Taking her hand, he placed it on the initials, stitched in small white thread: R.P. "You'll have to sign your own quilt, Faith," he said, his voice soft and soothing.

"I don't know what to say," she whispered. "I hadn't noticed..."

He smiled, a soft and kind smile. But he didn't speak. Instead, he pulled her closer, glancing once over his shoulder to make certain none of the children had come upstairs after them. He put an arm around her, holding her against his chest, her fingers still entwined with his. "You called me Manny," he said. "You haven't called me Manny in years."

Lowering her eyes, she felt the color flood to her cheeks. "I did, didn't I?"

She felt his finger touch her chin, tilting her head up so that he could look into her eyes. "You did, ja," he whispered before leaning down to gently press his lips against hers. The kiss was soft and sweet yet hinted at a longing on both of their parts. When he pulled away, he smiled and squeezed her hand. "Best get back downstairs, then," he said.

It took her a moment to catch her breath. She felt as if she had fire in her veins. When he released her hand and started toward the door, she could barely move. Her knees felt weak and she took a moment to compose herself. She looked back at the quilt, studying it as she breathed deeply. Rebecca's quilt, she thought. He moved it upstairs...How could she not have noticed that?

"Look Faith! I'm using the material from our dresses for my wedding quilt!" Rebecca grabbed Faith by the hand and led her into the back room of her mamm's house. She had told Faith that she was going to start her quilt when she turned sixteen. For her birthday, her parents had given her a cedar hope chest and Rebecca wasn't about to let it stay empty for long.

The quilting frame was set up near the window. It was empty at the moment for Rebecca hadn't finished piecing the quilt top. However, fabric was strewn atop it and Rebecca picked up pieces to show Faith. "Remember this dress? It's the floral one that you were wearing when we met!"

"Where did you get that?" Faith asked, laughing as she fingered the soft material.

"I asked your mamm!"

Clever girl, Faith thought but knew better than to praise Rebecca directly. She didn't like being praised.

"And this one..." She touched a pale pink fabric. "Remember that?"

Faith frowned. "It's Amish. That's not mine."

Laughing, Rebecca nodded her head. "Oh ja! It's my dress that you wore when I made you dress up Amish! We both wore that one!"

248

It amazed Faith that Rebecca had incorporated that dress into the wedding quilt. She was touched by the gesture, so typical of Rebecca who included her friend in everything that she did. "I don't know what to say," Faith managed. "It will be beautiful, that's for certain."

Rebecca glanced at the fabric again. "I think so, ja," she replied, the closest thing to pride that had ever crossed her lips. "Just think," she added turning to Faith. "Part of you will be on my marriage bed, too!"

It was the following morning when Manuel surprised her by bringing in the quilting frame from where he had stored it in the barn. He smiled at her, a sheepish smile, as he carried it through the kitchen and into the large, empty gathering room that would be used for church worship when it would be hosted at their home. She set Ruthie down on the floor and followed him into the room.

"What on earth!"

"It's your quilting frame," he replied.

She laughed. "I know what it is! What I'd like to know is why you are setting it up in here!"

"Vell," he said, lifting his hat off of his head and using the back of his wrist to wipe his brow. "You can't get started on our wedding quilt if it's not set up, ain't so?"

Faith frowned, eyeballing the wooden frame. "I don't know how to quilt!"

"Ja, I figured you'd say that so I invited Lydia to come over this week to get you started." The mischievous gleam in his eyes made it impossible to be upset with him.

"Manny!" she said, pretending to be upset but, when he

laughed at her, she found herself smiling.

She helped him set up the frame, thankful that there was a window in the room. It looked strange, set up in the large, empty room with nothing in it. There were a few folding chairs in the corner but, besides that, the room was barren. She couldn't imagine all of the church benches lined up and the people of the church district gathered for worship in their home.

When they returned to the kitchen, Ruthie was trying to crawl up the stairs. Faith hurried over to pick her up and carried her back toward the sofa. Setting her back on the floor, Faith redirected the baby's attention to the pots she had put down for the six month old to play with.

"How long will it take to make a quilt, Manny?"

He shrugged, leaning against the kitchen counter and watching her as she began washing the dishes. "Depends, I guess, on the pattern and how many women come to help you."

"Women?"

He nodded, reaching out to brush back a piece of her hair that had snuck free from her bun. "That's what a quilting bee is," he explained. "Surely you know that."

"I have to invite women here?" The thought terrified her. She had never entertained anyone, never had a reason to do so. She had always lived at home with her parents and any entertaining had been orchestrated by her mother.

His finger brushed along her neck and he moved closer to her. "You can do that, Faith," he said, lowering his voice. "You need to get to know the women in the g'may," he explained. He let his hand linger on her shoulder and smiled, too aware of how uncomfortable she felt. "They are part of our family, too." He paused before adding. "Your family...now that you are my wife."

"Manuel," she whispered.

There was a look in his eye, a look that spoke of what he was feeling inside. She felt her chest rise and fall as her breath quickened in his presence. There was something about him, something about how he touched her, his skin on hers, that caught her off guard.

The children were at school and Ruthie was busy with her toys. With the exception of the baby, they were alone. Yet, Faith felt conflicted, nervous about being with Manuel when he had that look in his eye and she felt her blood racing through her veins.

"I...I can't," she said and looked away, ashamed that she would deny him this.

"Ssssh." He pulled her close and wrapped his arms around her. "I know, Faith. We aren't ready yet."

She leaned her cheek against his shoulder, shutting her eyes and just taking in the moment. His arms felt warm and strong, comforting and safe. She breathed deeply, smelling the musky scent of his skin through the fabric. "I..." She stumbled over her words, unable to say what she was feeling.

"You what, Faith?"

She pulled back and lifted her eyes to look at him. "I...I want to be your wife, Manny," she said, feeling the heat in her cheeks. "But I just can't. Not yet."

He nodded. "I understand. One day," he started. "One day we will both feel comfortable."

"I just feel like it would be a betrayal," she whispered. "Is that wrong?"

He touched her cheek, his fingers light and soft against her skin. "I don't think anything you feel is wrong, Faith." He leaned down and pressed his lips against her forehead. "We just have to have faith in God that He will lead us to be together when it is right."

She nodded her head. "I do believe that, Manuel," she said solemnly. "I feel it in my heart and soul." But that wasn't it. No, it was Rebecca, she wanted to say. It was the memory of Rebecca that haunted her. To truly become Manuel's wife felt like being disloyal to Rebecca. She glanced at Ruthie who was sitting on the floor, a plastic spoon in her hand. "I know that Rebecca wanted this for her children. The question that still lingers," she said, returning her gaze to Manuel's face. "Is whether Rebecca wanted this for her *husband*."

He nodded, empathetic to her concern. "I understand. But you must remember that she walks with God while you are now my wife. I am *your* husband now." He lifted her hand to his lips, brushing her skin gently with a soft kiss. "It's going to be fine, Faith. We will give it time," he said, finally taking a step backward. "And we have plenty of that, Faith."

Time. She nodded her head, appreciative of his understanding. Just the night before, she had fought back tears and he had held her, comforting her until she fell asleep in his arms. She felt such a conflict of emotions, the weight of them far too heavy on her heart.

Chapter Fourteen

It was two days later when Lydia stopped into the Petersheim's farm, a brown bag under her arm and a smile on her face. "I must say," she announced when she walked into the kitchen. "I've missed your company, Faith!"

Faith laughed. "Me, too," she admitted.

"And your help in the evening with those kinner," Lydia said, shaking her head. "I don't know how I did it before, without you!"

They visited over a cup of coffee for the next thirty minutes, Lydia sharing family news with her despite Faith not knowing all of the names that were mentioned. One thing that Faith had learned long ago, while visiting at Rebecca's house as a child, was that a social visit from any Amish person always turned into an amazingly elaborate lesson in genealogy.

Before long, Lydia glanced at the clock on the wall and reached for the bag that she had brought with her. "Best get started picking out a pattern, ja?" She reached into the bag and pulled out a stack of papers, each one a different size and with a photograph of a quilt on it. "You look through these and see if you find something that strikes your fancy," Lydia said, pushing the papers toward Faith. "I think it's wunderbaar that you want to make a quilt for you and Manuel. And quilting bees in the winter are always a right gut time."

Faith looked through the different photos of quilts, her mind in a whirl at the monstrous task ahead of her. "I don't know why Manuel thinks I can do this," she mumbled. "How on earth am I to piece the quilt top?"

Lydia laughed. "You send it out to have someone do it, Faith!" She shook her head and said, "Did he tell you that you were to piece it, then? He's such a teaser, that one."

Even Faith had to smile.

She was halfway through the pile when her eyes fell on a pattern that jumped at her. It was simple and sweet yet beautiful at the same time. "This one," she said, sliding the card across the table toward Lydia. "This is the one that I'd like."

Lydia nodded her approval. "The double wedding ring," she said. "How appropriate."

"I think in blues, don't you?"

"That would be quite lovely, I'm sure. You'll have to go pick out some fabrics before we take it to the Lapp sisters to piece it." Lydia glanced again at the clock. "Oh help," she said. "Good thing you found a pattern you like right quick! We visited so long that we best get going to the store if we're to return in time for making dinner." She started to get up but hesitated. "Do you have any quilting supplies? We'll need thread for certain but what about pins and needles?"

Faith nodded. "I think I saw a sewing box near the Singer machine in the grossdaadihaus. Let me go check," she said and hurried through a doorway into the smaller house that was attached by a breezeway.

With no one living there, Rebecca must have done her sewing in the grossdaadihaus, liking the different views of the farm from the back windows. Faith paused, looking outside and seeing Manuel spreading manure on the fields behind the house. The large Belgian mules were pulling the spreader as he guided them down the field. His straw hat fell from his head and, as Faith watched, Manuel stopped the mules to retrieve it. He glanced down at the house, just for a brief moment, before he returned to his chores.

Smiling to herself, Faith reached down for the sewing box that was, indeed, beside the sewing machine. She set it atop the small table and opened the lid to see what was inside in order to report back to Lydia. As the lid fell backward, a long white envelope fell to the floor. Faith frowned as she bent down to pick it up. An envelope? She turned it over and, as her eyes fell upon the single word written on the front, she gasped.

Faith.

Her hands began to tremble and her eyes darted back to the window, seeking out Manuel in the field. She didn't have to open the envelope to know who had written her name on the front. The handwriting was unmistakable: Rebecca's handwriting. Her heart pounded inside of her chest and she felt dizzy as she stared at her name.

Why would Rebecca have written a letter for her? Why would she have put it in her quilting box? She tried to open the envelope but her hands were shaking too hard. Stunned, she quickly sat down in the nearest chair. A letter from the grave, she thought, her eyes immediately tearing. Taking a deep breath, she shut her eyes and said a silent prayer, which took the edge off of her nerves, allowing her to slip her finger under the envelope's lip in order to slide it open.

My dearest friend, Faith,

If you are reading this letter, I imagine you are standing in the grossdaadihaus, having gone to retrieve my sewing kit. It's a thought that pleases me for I can only presume that you are tending to my kinner.

I can picture you in my mind, wearing a green or

burgundy dress and a white heart-shaped prayer cover. I like to think of you that way, just like when we were children.

The doctors told me after that last miscarriage that I have something known as endometriosis. I think you are familiar with that condition for your own mamm had it.

The doctors warned me to not have more children but, as you can see, I did. How could I deny Manuel the family that he so deserves? Every man lives for a large family, for passing on his faith and love to grandchildren and great-grandchildren.

I made the decision to let God decide what was best for my family.

You see, if you are reading this letter, I am walking with Jesus and you are tending to my family. And I know this because you made me a promise to do just that. I haven't forgotten that promise and I know that you wouldn't either. That's the type of friendship we have.

I feel so blessed to be able to share my family with you, Faith. You were always one that needed a family. You just didn't know it. Love my family, Faith. All of them. It's my dying wish to know that, not only my kinner will have the next best thing to their mamm, but that my husband will have his large family. Even a larger one that the one I gave him.

Danke, Faith. No matter what has happened, just know that I love you and will forever be grateful for what you have given to me...peace of mind as I go to walk with God.

With love and many blessings,

Rebecca

Faith sat there, shocked as her eyes scanned over the neatly spaced, handwritten words. Endometriosis? Rebecca had known that she shouldn't have children, rather than couldn't have them? She had known that, while the condition itself was painful but not death threatening, if she were to carry a child to term there could be complications during delivery and she might very well die? She knew this yet she had chosen to hide her medical condition from everyone out of love for her husband. Her eyes lifted to the window, gazing at the field one last time and watching as Manuel turned the mules and the spreader to continue on the next row.

Her mind reeled and she lifted her hand to her forehead, feeling a surreal feeling of confusion overcome her. The promise. The request for Faith at the bedside during labor. The final words. Rebecca had orchestrated everything, hand-selecting a new wife for her husband and a mamm for her kinner. Certainly, she hadn't known that the baby would live...it was a chance that she had taken when she had refused to have a hysterectomy and proceeded to become pregnant once again.

"Oh Rebecca," she whispered, tears falling from her eyes. "What have you done?"

"Faith?"

She glanced over her shoulder as Lydia peeked through the door.

"Did you find it, then?"

Faith wiped at her eyes and nodded her head. "I did, Lydia. And something more." She lifted the piece of paper in her hand, trying to stop the flow of tears. "A letter."

Lydia frowned and walked into the room. "A letter? To

whom?"

"Me."

"To you?" Lydia looked confused. "From whom?"

"Rebecca."

Lydia gasped, the color draining from her cheeks.

Faith glanced at the letter that she still held in her hands. "I...I have to go talk to Manuel," she said. "This needs to be shared with him."

"Of course, of course." If Lydia was curious about the contents of the letter, she never asked. Instead, she quietly excused herself, leaving Faith to re-read the letter one more time in the quiet of the grossdaadihaus. Five minutes later, she heard the buggy heading out the driveway as Lydia was leaving the farm.

Faith shut her eyes and tried to picture Rebecca writing this letter. Had she written it while seated at the kitchen table, her belly swollen with her unborn child? Why had she placed the letter in the sewing box? How had she known that Faith would, indeed, find it?

She waited until Ruthie went down for her late morning nap before she grabbed her black shawl from the hook on the wall. Wrapping it around her shoulders, she glanced in the mirror by the front door, pausing for just a moment to pinch her cheeks and smooth back her hair. She had spent the past hour trying to make sense of the letter and what Rebecca had done. While Ruthie fussed and played, Faith had paced the floor, unable to comprehend the sacrifice that Rebecca had made for her husband. She toyed with the idea of not sharing it with him, wondered whether he truly needed to know. Yet, she knew that a good marriage was one that kept no secrets.

Once outside, she caught her breath against the cold air. It stuck to her lungs and left her breathless as she hurried to the barn. It was warm inside the barn and she sat on a hay bale, waiting for almost twenty minutes before she heard the familiar plodding of the mules' large hooves on the driveway and the rattle of the spreader's wheels. She could see him pass the doorway as he led the mules to their stalls, located on the other side of the barn. She waited for another five minutes, her heart pounding and her hands still shaking.

"Faith!"

She looked up and stared at him when he said her name. He had already unhitched the mules and had been walking through the barn to go to the house for dinner. Clearly, he hadn't expected to see her sitting in the barn.

"I thought you were going out with Lydia," he said, walking toward her. "Is everything OK?"

She nodded but couldn't speak.

"What is it? What's wrong?"

She reached for his hand and, when he took her hand, she stood before him, her eyes searching his face. She could see confusion in his blue eyes, the edges wrinkling just a touch as he tried to elicit an answer from her. But she couldn't say a word. Instead, she reached out her other hand and touched his cheek, her eyes wide and bright.

"Faith?"

She shut her eyes for a moment, swallowed hard and whispered. "I'm scared, Manny."

He tilted her chin so that she was forced to look at him. His blue eyes searched her face, trying to understand what was bothering her. Yet, he could find no indication of its source.

"What is it, Faith? What has happened?"

"I'm scared," she said, her words barely audible. She didn't know how to say what she was feeling, how Rebecca's letter had created an urgency in her. The desire to complete what was started on the day that she had agreed to marry him. "I'm so scared."

He frowned, concerned. "Scared of what, Faith?"

"I'm scared to take that step and become your wife," she admitted, praying that he didn't think of her as being too brazen and forward. But she knew that she needed to speak her mind, to let him know what she was feeling. "Scared to be your real wife in all ways." She paused, biting her lower lip as she held his gaze. His beautiful blue eyes stared into hers, confused by her admission but quietly waiting for her to continue. "But I'm ready, Manuel. It's time."

For a moment, he looked stunned by her words. She worried that he would take her admission the wrong way, think she was too forward and brazen. He took a sharp intake of breath and studied her expression. "What is this about, Faith?"

She felt weak and knew that if he didn't put his arms around her, if he didn't hold her, she risked falling as her knees felt weak. "Please, Manny," she pleaded softly, begging him with her eyes. She reached for his hand and pressed her cheek against it. "I...I need to be your wife. In all ways. I need this. Need to do this." She continued to stare up at him. "No, not need. Want. I want to be your wife."

Stroking her cheek, he kept staring into her face. His eyes softened and she saw him swallow, the only indication that he was as nervous as she felt. Surely he was curious as to what had happened, what had brought this about so suddenly.

But he didn't ask. Instead, he nodded his head.

"I want you to be my wife, too," he replied softly.

He lowered his hand from her cheek and reached out for her to take his hand, entwining his fingers within hers. Without another word, they walked back to the house together. When he stood before the door, he paused and looked at her, a tenderness in his face as he proceeded to lift her hand to his lips and kiss the back of her fingers. When she lowered her eyes, ignoring the pounding of her heart inside of her chest, he slowly opened the door and stepped back as he waited for her to walk inside before him.

It was later that evening, after the children had gone upstairs to bed, that Faith finally had the courage to approach Manuel. When he looked up at her, he smiled and reached out his hand. Timidly, she placed her small hand in his and blushed when he kissed her palm. His lips against her skin sent delicious shivers up her spine and she smiled to herself. How different she felt, she realized. One letter, one afternoon, one moment...it changed everything.

"Manny," she said softly, hating to break the moment but knowing that she had to tell him about the letter. "I...I need to show you something."

He pulled on her hand so that she slipped over the arm of the chair and onto his lap. Wrapping his arms around her, he nuzzled at her neck. "What could that be, Faith?"

Shutting her eyes, she couldn't help herself from enjoying his affection. She shuddered, a wave of tingles traveling up her spine and a warm feeling washing all over her. Earlier, after she had approached him in the barn, he had led her through the kitchen, pausing one last time outside of their bedroom door. He had looked at her, as if making certain that this was what she had wanted: to become his wife in all aspects. Her heart had pounded inside of her chest, her blood pulsating through her veins. Despite her fears and trepidation, she had nodded and, still holding his hand, quietly followed him through the doorway.

It was much later, when Ruthie awoke, that she noticed a new sense of intimacy between them. They had been standing by the kitchen window, his body leaning toward her as they simply stared at each other. His blue eyes sparkled and he smiled when she blushed. As her cheeks reddened, he had leaned forward to brush his lips against hers, a soft and tender communication that defied the need for any words.

That was when the baby began to cry. Manuel smiled and reached for her hand, lifting it to press his lips against her skin. "Let's get her together, ja?" he had asked and, not waiting for an answer, started walking toward the stairs. Indeed, for the rest of the afternoon, Manuel had lingered around the house, never more than a few feet from Faith who took special comfort in his presence.

Yet the letter had lingered in her mind and she knew she had to share it with Manuel. She needed him to know the truth about Rebecca's death and their subsequent marriage.

So now, as she sat on his lap, his arms wrapped around her, she took a deep breath and began. "Manny," she started. "Something happened today."

"Ja," he murmured. "Something wunderbaar happened today, indeed."

She tried not to smile at the hidden meaning in his response. "I'm being serious."

"And I hope it happens again later tonight..."

"Manuel!"

Sensing the change in her tone, Manuel leaned back, quickly assessing her expression. "What is it, Faith? Does this have to do with your change of heart?"

She nodded. "I found something in the grossdaadihaus. Something that I think you should look at." She wiggled off of his lap and walked over to the cabinet where she had placed the letter, safe from curious eyes. It felt heavy in her hands as she crossed back to where he sat, watching her. "I found this next door in Rebecca's quilting box. Lydia had wanted me to see what quilting supplies I would need before we left for the store. After I read it..." She paused. How could she explain this? How could she explain that the message from his deceased wife, her best friend, had removed the last barrier to their marriage? "Well, I think when you read it, you'll understand."

And then she handed him the letter.

It took a moment for him to comprehend what he was holding in his hands. He looked up at Faith, their eyes meeting for a long second, before he turned his attention back to the piece of paper in his hands. She watched as he opened the folded paper and his eyes darted over each word, so neatly written. Faith caught her breath when she saw him cringe and shut his eyes, the color draining from his face. At one point, he rubbed at his face and shook his head. More than anything, Faith wished she knew what he was thinking as he digested Rebecca's message from the grave.

"Mein Gott," he murmured when he had finally finished reading it. He looked up at Faith, the hint of tears in his eyes. "I had no idea."

Faith took a deep breath, a wave of relief flooding over

her. "I didn't think you knew." The idea that Manuel had known about Rebecca's condition had lingered over her mind. Indeed, she hadn't been certain of how she would have handled that information should he have admitted that he knew and proceeded to support Rebecca trying to have more children. Now that she knew the truth, that Rebecca had kept that information from Manuel and traveled that path alone, she could breathe again. "But it explains so much to me."

He nodded thoughtfully. "Ja, it does." His eyes scanned the letter once again and Faith watched quietly. She could see that it began to dawn on him, the extent of what Rebecca had done. A frown creased his forehead and he glanced away, his eyes clouding over as he reached back into his memory. Something dawned on him and Manuel slowly turned his head to look at Faith. "She knew."

"She knew," Faith repeated.

He glanced at her, realizing that she had misunderstood him. Frustrated, Manuel shook his head. "Nee, I don't mean about the pregnancy but about *me*."

Now it was Faith's turn to frown. She had thought he meant that Rebecca knew that she would die and had willingly given her life in exchange for Ruthie's. With Manuel's words, Faith realized that he was focusing on something else "What about you?"

He shut his eyes and leaned back in his chair, struggling to find the right words. "Do you remember the pond? The day when you almost drowned?" When he paused, she nodded. "She knew how I felt about you after that happened."

How he felt about her? His words shocked Faith. "What are you saying, Manuel?"

He looked at the wall for a minute, his mind in a

whirlwind. She could tell from his expression that he was experiencing an inner struggle, while formulating a response. Patiently, she waited, giving him that time to clear his head. Finally, he stood up and began to pace the floor, the contents of the letter still in his thoughts. Mumbling some words in Pennsylvania Dutch, he shook his head before he stopped and turned toward Faith.

"It was after the pond incident," he said, lowering his voice. "I was always inquiring about you, asking how you were. It wasn't that I was interested in you, being Englische and all, but I felt…" He glanced in the air as if the words were lingering, there over his head. "Protective of you. Concerned about you." Lifting his hands to his head, he rubbed his temples. "I'll never forget that day, the day that I breathed life into you, Faith. It was both the scariest and the most exhilarating day of my life. I was so scared that you would drown, this pretty little soaking wet Mennonite girl. And when you came back, returned from near death, I wanted to cry with joy. Don't you see? I felt connected with you, Faith, even then."

Even then.

He looked at her, his eyes fierce and alive as if he had just had a great revelation. "I *knew* we'd always be connected. You can't save someone's life without feeling that bond." His eyes fell onto the paper in his hand, a look of wonder on his face. "She knew that, too, and when she knew what was going to happen to her, she pushed us toward each other. She prepared for the future of her family by insuring that you would be the one to take care of us." He shook his head, not quite comprehending what he had just learned. "She pushed us together, didn't she?"

Faith stood before him, reaching to hold his hands. She

didn't want this revelation to create a barrier between them with their newfound relationship. No, that had not been her intention. In fact, she had felt that he needed to know and understand the reasons behind Faith's change in attitude toward her marriage. "She pushed us, yes," Faith started, fighting back the tears that threatened to cloud her vision and wet her cheeks. "But it's God who opened our eyes, isn't it, Manuel? God made this possible and He made love happen between us."

He stopped when he heard what she said and sharpened his gaze. For a long moment, he studied her face before he squeezed her hands and repeated the word that she had just spoken. "Love?"

The way that he said the word caused the color to flood to her cheeks again. Had she misread his signs? Had she jumped too quickly? "Well," she stammered. "I meant at least from me to you and the children."

"You love me?" He seemed surprised to have heard those words from her lips.

"Oh Manny," she whispered, wiping at her eyes so that a tear wouldn't roll down her cheek. "How could I not?"

This time, he shut his eyes and a hint of a smile crossed his lips. That look of peace fell over his face once again and she felt her heart swell. "Oh Faith," he whispered back. "I will pray my thanks to God for truly it's better to have love given back than just received."

His response puzzled her. "I don't understand," she managed to say.

"Faith," he said, quickly opening his eyes and staring at her. "Don't you know how I feel about you? How much I love you, too? You saved me. You saved my family. You have returned life and love and happiness to this house. And by doing so, you have that forever bond with me...the same way that I have a forever bond with you."

"Forever," she whispered, the idea of eternity causing her to catch her breath. "And this was Rebecca's gift to us, wasn't it?"

"She had to do what she felt was right," he agreed. He leaned forward, pressing his forehead against hers as he clutched her hands in his. "But, in doing so, she made certain that all of her loved ones were taken care of. It was a brave and selfless decision."

Faith wasn't certain of how she felt about the word *selfless*. She was fairly sure that, if given the choice two years back, the kinner would have argued for Rebecca to not take that chance, to avoid getting pregnant in order to live. However, when Faith thought about sweet Ruthie and her toothless smiles and babyish laughter, she wondered what the kinner would think now. A question, she realized, that no one would ever dare to ask. Nor should they.

Shutting her eyes, Faith took a deep breath. "Selfless in that she gave her own life in order for the rest of us to have one. Only our lives are not more important than hers, are they?"

He nodded his head. "I reckon you are right," he admitted. "But she had her reasons for doing what she did. She felt it was the right thing, that God would guide her. And she wanted to know that, if He took her home, her family was provided for. In that regard, she was selfless, ja?"

He wrapped his arms around her, pulling her to his chest and holding her tightly. For a long moment, she shut her eyes and pressed her cheek against his shoulder. His embrace comforted her and removed any lingering doubts over the decision she had made to step into the lives of the Petersheim family and take over where Rebecca had left off. Their union had the blessing of God as well as the understanding, support, and guiding hand of Rebecca.

Chapter Fifteen

Faith stood in the back of the schoolhouse, close enough to Manuel to feel his presence without actually touching each other. It wouldn't be proper to hold hands or lean against him at the winter recital. But knowing that he was there gave her great comfort.

The children were standing at the front of the school, dressed in their Sunday best as they sang the Christmas hymns for their parents to enjoy. Their cherubic voices and bright eyes warmed Faith's heart. She listened to the songs, having practiced with Sadie and Benjamin at home so that, when it came time for the pageant, she would better understand the words to the songs as the children performed them.

She leaned back and turned her head so that her lips were close to Manuel's ear. "Look how happy she is," she whispered, indicating the broad smile on Sadie's face.

He placed his hand on her hip, a subtle gesture that no one else could see as he responded, "Her new mamm is here. She's quite proud, don't you think?"

Faith nodded, trying to hide her own smile of pride. It had been almost a month since she had married Manuel, a month of joy and bliss. Each day was more remarkable than the last. She found joy in tending to the house and the chores. What's more, she found a sense of peace in loving Manuel and the kinner. While Rebecca was never far from Faith's mind, she knew that everyone was moving on so that life could continue, as both God and Rebecca wanted.

Looking across the room, she smiled at Anna who stood

with the older girls at the back of the school. Anna was holding Ruthie, the eight month old staring at the singing children in amazement. It was the first time Ruthie was in a schoolhouse and the first time she heard children singing without adults. She was mesmerized by the sounds.

It was a Friday, the last day of school before the winter break and holiday season. The Christmas service had been held the previous week on Sunday. It had been a regular worship service with very limited discussion of the Holy Birth, unlike the services that Faith had been familiar with at her Mennonite church.

Their own family gathering would be held the following Sunday. Faith was nervous about attending her first Christmas dinner with all of the Petersheim family. With all of the children and grandchildren, there would be over a hundred people at the dinner. Her own parents were also invited and for that, Faith was most grateful. She hadn't seen much of them since her decision to join the church and marry Manuel. Her life had taken a turn with so many responsibilities and chores around the farm and home.

After the pageant, there was a light fellowship in the schoolhouse. Families had bought fresh bread and cold cuts, chow-chow and pickled beets, applesauce and fresh pies. It was a nice end of the week treat to visit with the families and friends of the children before the holiday weekend.

The sky was dark when the family walked home together, Sadie and Benjamin holding Faith's hands as Manuel carried Ruthie, bundled in a coat and blanket, in his arms. Behind them, Gideon and Mary walked together while Anna lingered with some of her friends. Faith glanced back, seeing the battery operated lantern swinging gently in Anna's hands and, to her delight, noticed Jonas Zook walking with the girls. *That will make Anna's Christmas*, Faith thought with a smile.

Back at the house, Faith helped the younger children take off their coats and scarves, hanging them on the pegs from the wall in the washroom before she removed her own black bonnet and wrap. "I think that was a lovely pageant," she said as she smoothed back her hair to make certain it was under her kapp before she walked into the kitchen. "Perhaps we should celebrate with some popcorn and games?"

Sadie and Benjamin cheered.

"Chokinole?" Benjamin asked, his eyes wide and eager.

Manuel shifted Ruthie in his arms and rubbed her back. "That sounds like a good game, ja!"

Sadie frowned. "But only four can play at a time!"

Faith laughed. "We can take turns, goose."

Benjamin hurried to the backroom to find the large board game while Gideon and Mary cleared off the kitchen table. Faith watched them as she prepared an evening bottle for Ruthie. The baby was starting to drift to sleep in Manuel's arms, her eyelids drooping as she sucked on her thumb.

"Best be getting her changed and to bed," Faith said, offering to take Ruthie.

"I'll do it, Mamm," Anna offered. Without waiting for a response, Anna reached for the bottle and tucked it into her dress pocket before lifting the sleepy baby from her daed's arms. With a smile, Anna tucked the baby into the crook of her arm and hurried up the stairs.

Manuel and Faith glanced at each other, silently wondering about Anna's sudden enthusiasm to spend time with the baby. It was a knowing look that defied words, a look that could only be shared between two people that shared a special bond.

With the four children leaning over the Crokinole board, Faith turned her attention to making the popcorn. Pouring a little olive oil in the bottom of a pot, she waited for the propane stove to light and heat it before she poured in a thin layer of golden kernels.

"You know what you're doing there, then?" Manuel asked, leaning his hip against the counter as he watched her, a smile on his face and a twinkle in his eye.

"It's popcorn," she laughed. "I've made it dozens of times."

"You have now, have you?" he teased, leaning forward to brush his hand along her arm. She felt that familiar shiver race up her spine and shut her eyes for a second. "Show me what you are doing," he whispered as he stood behind her, his shoulder pressing against hers.

She tried not to smile but couldn't help it, especially when she felt her cheeks grow warm and she knew they had turned red. Manuel loved to make her blush and was getting quite good as doing so. "Well," she managed to say. "I heat up the olive oil before I put in a layer of the kernels."

She felt his finger on her neck and quickly glanced at the kitchen table. The children were absorbed in the game and hadn't noticed.

"What's next, Faith?"

"Well," she started. "It pops and then I put..." But she could tell that he wasn't interested in the popcorn for she had felt his breath on her skin and lost her concentration. "Manuel..."

"Hmmm?"

She turned around and found herself in his arms. He

was chuckling to himself and quietly brushed his lips against hers. Her eyes flickered to the table, relieved to see that the children were still battling with each other over who had crossed the black line before the button was put into play.

Manuel didn't seem to mind if the children had seen. Instead, he pulled her closer and leaned down. "I love you, Faith," he whispered in her ear, low enough so that the children couldn't hear.

"Oh," she managed to reply, startled by this unusual display of affection. While he had said it before, in actions during the day and in words in the privacy of their bedroom, he had never been so forthcoming with his emotions toward her.

He gave her one last kiss, soft and quiet, before he pulled away, just slightly, and mouthed, "Your popcorn..."

Indeed it was. "Oh help!" she exclaimed, realizing that the lid was beginning to rattle on the pot as the kernels of corn rose.

Manuel stepped away, laughing as Faith picked up the pot and shook it gently so that the kernels on the bottom wouldn't burn. She glanced at Manuel, pretending to frown at him as he watched her with an amused expression on his face.

"I think you distracted me on purpose," she teased.

"Mayhaps I did," he admitted. "But a nice distraction it was, ja?"

Taking a deep breath, she watched him as he smiled mischievously before turning his attention to the children playing the board game. Every so often, he would look up and catch her eye and let his gaze linger, just long enough to cause her cheeks to flush.

"Is that popcorn almost ready, then?" Gideon asked,

looking up from the game with a grin on his face. "I'm getting mighty hungry over here, beating Anna and Sadie at this game!"

"Me, too!" Benjamin chimed in, bouncing in his seat.

Faith laughed. "Ja, ja, just let me add the salt and Brewer's yeast." She took the pot over to the prepared bowl and opened the lid. To her surprise, a few kernels of corn popped out of the bowl. She jumped in surprise and the children laughed at her.

"Oh help!" she muttered as a few more kernels flew through the air and onto the floor.

"They always do that!" Sadie laughed, jumping up to help Faith by picking up the scattered pieces. "They like to startle you!"

"And they always do," Faith added, smiling her appreciation at the young girl. "Now help me salt this popcorn and then you can help me eat it!"

The rest of the evening was spent huddled over the Crokinole board, cheering and laughing as the family took turns playing the game. In the end, no one bothered to keep a final score. It wasn't who won the game that was important, after all. It was the fact that they spent the evening together, enjoying each other's company and being one as a family.

Epilogue

Faith covered her head with the end of the black shawl and wrapped the two ends around herself. She slipped out the side door of the kitchen and hurried down the driveway. Ruthie was sleeping and she knew that she only had a two-hour window of time.

She walked down the road, her head bent down as she thought and prayed. It had been just over four months since she had married Manuel. The winter was almost over, although she smelled snow in the air. The winter's last snowfall, she hoped.

It had been a light winter but Faith was tired of short days and ready for spring. She longed for flowers, open windows, and green leaves covering the trees. She yearned to bring picnic lunches to her husband while he worked in the fields, to lie in the grass with baby Ruthie who had just learned to crawl, and to work outside with the sun on her back.

But today, it was still winter.

When she finally approached the small plot of land surrounded by a black metal fence, she paused, taking a moment to collect her thoughts before she entered the graveyard. Today is a big day, she thought to herself as she carefully maneuvered through the rows of headstones and found the one with the name Rebecca Petersheim etched into it.

Faith hadn't been to the graveyard before that day. She had not returned since last April when Rebecca had died. Seeing the grave marker sent a chill through her spine. *That's*

Rebecca, she thought, fighting the urge to cry. *She's under there.*

For a moment, she felt a wind on her face and, despite the coldness in the air, a warmth spread throughout her body. She was no longer cold. *Rebecca,* Faith said to herself with a smile.

"You changed everything," Faith said out loud. "I'm not certain why you did this, Rebecca, and I won't say that I'm glad that you did it. But I wanted to tell you that everything is going to be fine. Your kinner are adapting and growing."

She paused to take a deep breath. It only felt right to continue talking to Rebecca, to tell her about her family. "Anna has become a fine young woman and has been a tremendous help to me. We're friends, Rebecca, but I keep you in mind when I guide her."

The familiar noise of a horse and buggy interrupted her, carried by the wind. Faith glanced up and saw a black horse pulling the grey-top buggy down the road. The driver lifted his hand to wave to her as he passed.

"Mary is so quiet and likes to crochet all of the time. You taught her well and, now, she's teaching me. Gideon is so much like his daed. He'll be a fine young man and be quite helpful to Manuel."

She laughed. "Sadie reminds me of you when we first met. She sure does have a lot of energy. Benjamin has a hard time keeping up with her. But they get on nicely and, when it becomes too much, Gideon steps in to help Benjamin."

Lifting her eyes to the sky, Faith found it hard to say the next part. Tears formed in her eyes and she wiped at them before she continued. "You never knew Ruthie. Ruthie was mine from the beginning, I reckon. You gave birth to her and they simply handed me the baby." A tear fell. "I'm sorry for that, Rebecca. You would have loved her so much, just as I do. She might limp a bit when she finally walks but she is the most cheerful baby, so full of love and grace."

A flake of snow fluttered down through the grey skies and landed on Faith's eyelash. "Thank you for choosing me to be her mamm," she whispered, wiping again at her eyes.

For a moment, she shut her eyes and breathed in the cold air. It stung her lungs and she began to feel chilled in her toes. She could hear another buggy approaching, the clip-clop of the horse's hooves on the macadam and the humming of the buggy announcing its presence.

It was getting colder and she needed to get back home. More snow was falling now, large flakes that were sticking on the ground. One more deep breath and Faith could finish what she came to say.

"I found your letter, Rebecca, and it was such a blessing. Your letter explained a lot, although I still have so many questions I would love to ask you. It removed any lingering doubts or concerns and for that, I thank you."

She smiled and touched her stomach. "I'm having a baby, Rebecca, the baby you always told me that I would have...the baby I never knew that I wanted," she said. "I haven't told Manuel yet. I wanted you to know first. After all, you *are* my bestest friend." She paused, her eyes staring at the grave. "Everything else might have changed but that never will," she added softly.

"Faith?"

She glanced over her shoulder and saw a horse and buggy by the gate. Manuel.

"What are you doing there? It's freezing! Let me take you home," he said, sliding open the buggy door and getting out so that he could help her.

Faith nodded, casting one parting look at the grave before she navigated her way back to where Manuel was waiting. He gave her a quizzical look but didn't ask why she had chosen to walk to the graveyard in the freezing cold with a snowstorm on the way.

"Where's Ruthie?" she asked as she shut the gate behind her.

"Sleeping still," he responded. "When I realized you weren't there, I looked around and saw you walking down the road. Wanted to come get you and make sure you were OK." She walked up to the buggy and stood before him. He raised an eyebrow and tilted his head. "Everything all right, then?"

She nodded, smiling and lowering her eyes. "I had something I wanted to tell Rebecca before I told you," she said shyly, the color creeping onto her cheeks. "I would tell you at home but I can't contain myself anymore, Manny."

He tilted his head and waited.

Lifting her eyes, she looked into his face, her dark eyes meeting his blue ones as she said, "We're going to have a baby."

His reaction surprised her. He caught his breath, a look of complete surprise on his face. "A baby?" He reached for her hands and held them in his. "You're certain?"

She laughed and nodded. "For sure and certain!"

"Oh Faith," he said, his voice soft and full of emotion. Not caring if anyone passed by and saw, he pulled her into his arms and hugged her. "What a blessing!" he whispered into her ear. When he pulled back, she was surprised to see tears in his eyes. "I am overjoyed," he said, his hands holding her face tenderly as he stared down into it. "What a blessing, indeed!"

"Sssh Faith! You have to be quiet!"

Faith frowned, flickering her flashlight around the room. "I am being quiet!" she insisted.

"No! Quieter!"

Mamm had made three Tupperware containers full of chocolate and red velvet Whoopie Pies for a family gathering the next day. Neither Rebecca nor Faith saw any harm in taste testing them a bit early. They had waited patiently until the house had quieted down before they snuck out of the bedroom upstairs and quietly tiptoed down the hallway toward the stairs.

They crept down the staircase, trying to avoid the third step that creaked and might awaken Rebecca's mamm. It was after ten o'clock and they would get a scolding for certain if they woke anyone. But those Whoopie Pies were calling out to them.

Once in the kitchen, Rebecca motioned for Faith to follow her toward the pantry. Their flashlights flickered around the room like a wild lightshow in the darkness as they hurried to claim their bounty.

"It's so dark down here!" Faith whispered as she bumped into a long wooden bench sticking out from under the kitchen table. She carried her little flashlight, which whipped around the room, casting a wobbly beam onto the offending piece of furniture. "Where did that come from?"

"Sssh! Be careful. You wake my mamm and we'll know it for sure!"

At the pantry, Rebecca slowly opened the door, cringing when it scraped against the bottom of the floor. It was open just enough that they could both squeeze through. Rebecca flashed her light around until she found the Tupperware.

"I want a red velvet one," Faith whispered.

"OK," Rebecca said as she reached for the container and opened it. "Here, these are the red ones."

A few minutes later, they were sitting on the floor, happily eating the forbidden Whoopie Pies. Rebecca flashed her light at Faith and snickered. "You have cream all over your face. You better wipe that or Mamm will notice and know!"

Faith swiped at her mouth with the back of the sleeve of her nightdress.

She loved sleepovers at Rebecca's house. Unlike her own home, Rebecca's house was lively and full of joy. Her mother always made delicious treats and the girls loved to sneak late night snacks when the house was finally quiet.

"You're my bestest friend," Rebecca suddenly said. "You won't ever forget that, will you, Faith?"

"Of course not!" Faith whispered back. "I can't because you keep reminding me!"

In the darkness, Rebecca rolled her eyes and nudged Faith with her arm. "I'm serious, Faith. And as my best friend, you have to tell me all of your secrets first! I better not find out the good stuff after anyone else!"

"Even my mother?"

Rebecca scoffed. "Of course!"

Faith sighed. "Ok then, I guess."

"Promise me!"

Here we go again, Faith thought but with a light heart. Rebecca loved to make certain Faith was onboard with all of her ideas and plans for the future. Whenever she had a new one, Faith was always made to promise to take the journey with her. "I promise," she said.

Rebecca smiled and stood up, reaching down to help

Faith to her feet. "A promise that shall never be broken," she said and gave Faith a quick, affectionate hug.

They put the Tupperware containers back on the shelf before taking the stealth journey back across the kitchen and up the stairs in order to return to bed. In the morning, they'd deal with any questions about the missing Whoopie Pies, taking their chances that Rebecca's mamm would be too busy to notice. Even if they were caught, the ramifications could never negate the memory of a secret journey to share a treat in the darkness, just Rebecca and Faith together, bestest of friends forever.

One More Thing...

I want to personally thank you for reading Amish Faith. The characters in this book took on a special and more spiritual meaning for me when I realized that, without knowing it, I was retelling the story of Jonathan and David. I encourage you to read I Samuel to revisit this story and how the love of friends can be so powerful strong.

If you enjoyed this book, I'd be very grateful if you'd post a short review on Amazon. Your support really does make a difference. Not only do I read all the reviews in order to see what you liked and how I can improve, but they are also a great source of motivation. When I hear from my readers and fans, it really makes me want to keep writing...just for you.

If you'd like to leave a review or see a list of my books on Amazon, simply click here. And don't forget to follow me on Facebook so that you can hear firsthand about new, upcoming releases.

With blessings,
Sarah Price
http://www.facebook.com/fansofsarahprice

About Sarah Price

The Preiss family emigrated from Europe in 1705, settling in Pennsylvania as the area's first wave of Mennonite families. Sarah Price has always respected and honored her ancestors through exploration and research about her family's history and their religion. At nineteen, she befriended an Amish family and lived on their farm throughout the years.

Twenty-five years later, Sarah Price splits her time between her home outside of New York City and an Amish farm in Lancaster County, PA where she retreats to reflect, write, and reconnect with her Amish friends and Mennonite family.

Find Sarah Price on Facebook and Goodreads!
Learn about upcoming books, sequels, series, and contests!

Contact the author at sarahprice.author@gmail.com.
Visit her weblog at http://sarahpriceauthor.wordpress.com or
on Facebook at www.facebook.com/fansofsarahprice.

CPSIA information can be obtained at www.ICGtesting.com
Printed in the USA
LVOW13s2002140913

352491LV00016B/809/P